Grace-Filled Seasons

By Lisa Jennings

Then the angel showed me the river of the water of life, bright as crystal, flowing from the throne of God and of the Lamb through the middle of the street of the city; also, on either side of the river, the tree of life with its twelve kinds of fruit, yielding its fruit each month. The leaves of the tree were for the healing of the nations. No longer will there be anything accursed, but the throne of God and of the Lamb will be in it, and his servants will worship him. They will see his face, and his name will be on their foreheads.
—Revelation 22:1–4 ESV

Grace-Filled Seasons
© 2023 by Lisa Jennings

This title is also available in Kindle format.

Published with help from 100X Publishing
Olympia, Washington | www.100Xpublishing.com

ISBN: 979-8-9856830-4-2

Dedication

This book is dedicated to Jesus, my Lord and Savior, and all the people who walked with me through my seasons of life. The highs, lows, and everything in between, your love and faithfulness has been not only a comfort but an agent of change for personal growth and freedom.

Your love for God is like a north star pointing me in the right direction when circumstances longed to veer me off course.

Thank you for helping this ordinary girl see God 's extraordinary in every winter, spring, summer, and fall.

Table of Contents

Introduction

Grace-Filled Seasons is an adventure of God's amazing grace. These stories were carefully selected from my decade long blog called "My Sentimental Journey"—an ordinary girl's walk with an extraordinary God. Birthed out of heartbreak, during a season of walking with my mother and brother suffering dementia at the same time, my blog became a way to grapple with their declining health and an emerging relational landscape shift of becoming the only surviving member of my family.

Finding solace in God, I wrote to process grief, to preserve my family memories, and to press into the God of all comforts. Those ten years of blogging became a spiritual springboard of hope, seeing miracles out of all life's messes, and God's promises overshadowing the pain in every situation. Deep sorrow and *why* questions danced with joy with God's overwhelming love song of abounding grace. God is present in life's storms no matter how raging they may be, speaking peace and comfort in our chaos and bringing joy in the morning. What started me on a journey of trying to learn how to live with loss turned into learning how to fully live in every season covered and redeemed under the umbrella of His glorious grace and limitless joy.

So, I humbly present to you a collection of my blog posts, old and new, organized (by seasons) in a 52-week journey of finding God's all-sufficient grace through the year. Whether it's the dead of winter, the hope of spring, the warmth of summer, or the beauty of fall, *Grace-Filled Seasons* provides 12 easy-to-read stories for each season. It is filled with scriptures, quotes and a place to ponder after each section. My prayer for you is to find hope for whatever season you are facing. May you be encouraged by this ordinary girl's walk with our extra-ordinary God.

Celebrate God all day, every day. I mean reveal in him!
—Philippians 4:4 MSG

(Here's the first introduction to my blog in December of 2012.)

How beautiful on the mountains are the feet of those who bring good news, who proclaim peace, who bring good tidings, who proclaim salvation, who say to Zion, "Your God reigns!" —Isaiah 52:7 NIV

Beautiful feet? I can honestly say I've never looked at mine and declared that.

You see, in the flesh, they are wide and my toes are a tad on the stubby side. When placed alongside friends for a photo after my first pedicure, they quite resemble Fred Flintstone's feet (AKA Twinkle Toes). They'd be perfectly capable of pounding the dusty road with Barney Rubble after they lifted their prehistoric vehicle on route to Mr. Slate's rock quarry.

But God's Word is talking about feet that travel to share His good news—dusty, grimy feet that ran to declare captivity is over, that freedom is on its way.

Those formally offensive and disgraceful feet become messengers of hope, peace, and the promise of a new beginning. That's my hope and prayer for you today, that somehow these soiled, chubby feet will aid in declaring God's good news to you, proclaiming His peace in every one of your challenging situations. May your heart swell with joy at the good tidings God has for you. His love touches every hurt, fear, and heartbreak. "Your God reigns," and that truth deserves a hallelujah, and If I might, a yabba-dabba doo!"

My beloved speaks and says to me:
"Arise, my love, my beautiful one and come away, for behold, the
winter is past; the rain is over and gone. The flowers appear on the
earth the time of singing has come, and the voice of the turtledove
is heard in our land. The fig tree ripens its figs, and the vines are
in blossom; they give forth fragrance. Arise, my love, my beautiful
one, and come away."—Song of Solomon 2:10-13 ESV

"Winter is an etching, spring a watercolor, summer an oil painting
and autumn a mosaic of them all." —Stanley Horowitz

"Grace grows best in winter."
—Edith Clarkson

This Little Light of Mine

Through the years during Christmas time, my mom would buy me a special ornament, a little something that caught her fancy, which in turn hoped to catch mine. Whether it be whimsical or festive, they were always tokens of her love. At times, those tokens were presented by hand, lightly wrapped in tissue, tied up with a bow of mother's excitement. On other occasions, I would find them lying on my canopy bed, concealed in the small bag they were purchased in...eager to surprise me. These memories sparked a fondness for ornaments that carried into adulthood, kindling a desire to continue this tradition with my own children.

Each year we added to our family collection through thrift store finds or clearance bins, being continually delighted in each new addition.

However, regardless of our vast assortment to choose from, when it came time to decorate the tree, one ornament out shined them all: a small golden house with intricately cut out windows and doors. All in all, it was a rather simple ornament with no grand history to tell of its origin. Somehow it became the boys' most coveted treasure. They were always eager to awaken it from the slumbering storage box keeping it safe. Then, with even greater anticipation, they beamed with honor to nestle it among the tree boughs.

From day one I marveled at their exuberance over this seemingly less-than-showy bobble. When surrounded with an array of grander, glitzier ornaments, it appears to be completely obscure; easily overlooked and underrated by the average curious onlooker. Nevertheless, our boys immediately recognized its hidden potential at first glance. Their tiny hands cradling the delicately crafted ornament, they would place a miniature bulb inside, causing luminous light to spill through each opening. Thus, this once dark vessel was now aglow with warm splendor.

Though that was many years ago, seeing through their eyes this uncovered gem made me see its worth to a greater depth. Still to this day, this jewel continues to shine brightly, faithfully stirring our hearts with its simple wonder. One day years later, while thrift store shopping, our son Trent by chance found the exact same ornament. With great joy he purchased it to give to his brother Derek to celebrate his first Christmas in his own home.

Besides all the warm memories that flood my thoughts when I gaze upon that wondrous ornament, Matthew chapter 5 comes to mind:

You are the light of the world. A city set on the hill cannot be hidden. Nor do people light a lamp and put it under a basket,, but on a stand, and it gives light to all in the house. In the same way, let your light so shine before others, so that they may see your good works and glorify your Father in heaven. —Matthew 5:14-16 ESV

You, my friend, are a light! Esteemed with value, you have been curiously and intricately wrought from the hands of your adoring Creator, Almighty God. You have not been overlooked, rather uniquely fashioned to shine brightly and with purpose. Matthew 5:16 in the Message Bible says, "Shine! Keep open house; be generous with your lives. By opening up to others, you'll prompt people to open up with God, this generous Father in Heaven."

My frame was not hidden from You when I was being formed in secret (and) intricately and curiously wrought (as if embroidered with various colors) in the depths of the earth (a region of darkness and mystery). —Psalm 139:15 AMPC

"The Word of God is a lamp by night, a light by day, and a delight at all times." —Charles H. Spurgeon

"God crowns us. Most people crown their Christmas trees with either an angel or a star. God uses both." —Max Lucado

Prayer:

Lord, we pray we see all of Your glory in our lives. Thank you for personally handpicking us to shine gloriously. May we choose to shine more brightly each day!

Lucky U

While anxiously waiting for my counseling appointment (which I had extended an olive branch for a family member to attend), my hopes were high to come to a peaceful resolution. It was time for the wise counseling of a professional to help repair the severed relationship, beginning the process of mending torn emotions to a place of strength and deeper healing. Like tiny tears of muscle that pave the way to increased muscle mass, so, too, our relationship would optimistically be built up.

As my upcoming appointment drew near the prayer of King David in Psalm 139:23-24 AMPC came to mind. "Search me thoroughly O God, and know my heart! Try me and know my thoughts. And see if there is any wicked or hurtful ways in me, and lead me in the way everlasting." I longed for my heart to stay on the course of truth joined hand and hand in love.

As the meeting came to a close, regretfully the outcome was not what we had hoped for. Deeply wrestling with discouragement, the ride home was somber. Feeling an intensified and rather profound sense of loss, 2012 was closing its chapter to more sorrow than I had bargained for: my mom's congestive heart failure and increasing dementia, while also mourning my only other sibling health challenges of Lewy Body Dementia. And now the golden thread of hope of restoration was severed, swaying frayed and raw, making the approaching holidays more poignant with overwhelming sadness and grief.

Upon arriving safely at home, I was greeted with a rousing welcome from my loving husband, thoughtful son and two exuberant and affectionate dogs, Buddy and Buttons. My soul and body instantly sank into a cozy place called home. Their listening ears slowly warmed my chilly spirits, thawing out the cold harsh situation.

Shortly after I got home, the phone rang; it was Lawrence the husband of my dear friend Lisa from high school. He was calling to plan a surprise for her birthday the following day. His cleverly devised plan was as follows: First, his limo driver would pick us up, then swing over to their house for the birthday girl, surprising her when she got inside with my unannounced presence. After that, it was time to drive to Lawrence's company party.

We had a great time! Photos were taken and hugs exchanged, then off my husband and I went for over a two-hour ride in the limo...all for free! Her husband's generosity extended beyond his lovely wife; it was a gift to Kevin and I as well.

It's safe to say that it had been well over 26 years since I'd yearned to ride in a limousine with my husband. For 21 of those years, we lived only on one income while I stayed home, homeschooling our two boys, coupon clipping, bargain hunting, and pinching pennies till they squealed. And I loved every minute of it. So honestly, limo desires got placed way back on the back burner, I forgot it was still a simmering dream.

However, God is mindful of our dormant dreams, His Word promises to give us the desires of our heart. The same joy of watching my precious friend's elation on her special day was also God's, as He watched our joy. He had a glorious celebration on our behalf.

This was truly a magical night of sparkling cider toasts, birthday gifts and photos. Riding in high style, we also toured Christmas lights, gazing at twinkling stars and city lights from the heights of Rocky Butte. Finishing our glorious night, we ate at the same Denny's where we first met after a church gathering, sharing French fries like we did 30 years ago. This wondrous adventure was fulfilled in a limo with the license plate "LUCKY U".

Perhaps you, too, are struggling with a painful hurt or loss. Do you feel like the chips are down and you're down on your luck? May I encourage today with the promise of a God who knows your heart and heartache. He is a God who binds up the brokenhearted, repairing and restoring them to wholeness. His favor and grace rests on the broken and downtrodden. So, whether you find yourself in a luxury limo ride or not, the Lord wants to bless you; He knows the secret petitions of your heart. This is certain: we serve a mighty God who daily loads His children with benefits. With this profound truth, I lift my glass of sparkling cider with a toast in honor of a very highly favored, blessed and LUCKY U!

Blessed (fortunate, prosperous, and favored by God) is the nation whose God is the LORD, The people whom He has chosen as His own inheritance. —Psalm 33:12 AMP

"Nothing feels blessed about being broken. In fact, certain circumstances in life hurt so intensely that we think we will never heal. But blessing can come in the wake of our being broken."
—Charles Stanley

Prayer:
Father God, thank you for all Your blessings. We know that "luck" is actually Your divine set ups, not merely happenstance. We praise You for a faith we can lean on; rock-solid faith, not tossed to and fro by the times, seasons or what can be said as a "lucky break." We are blessed, and we honor and give You glory for it.

Found Joy

When we positioned the desk in our bedroom, I had high hopes of it becoming a cozy nook for me to write and study God's Word. This snug creative and emotional getaway morphed into a clutter "catch all," invoking no sense of calm or creativity. Simply put, for two years I was tempted to lay unfolded clothes and disheveled stacks of paperwork on its handy, smooth surface. Sad to say, I yielded to this temptation repeatedly. Finally, on one particular day, I decided it was high time that the desk was returned to its former glory.

Now cleared of its jumbled confusion, it was off to the kitchen to fetch some hot tea. The cheery "JOY" mug with red lettering seemed like the perfect choice to steep my decaffeinated green tea. Plop went the teabag into the steaming hot water, while I swirled in tasty agave nectar.

Next on the list was to gather my Bible, devotionals and journal. Though I was able to find both my Bible and devotions rather quickly, my personal journal was nowhere to be found. My joy was now cooling as quickly as my once piping-hot cup of tea. "Where is it, Lord?" I asked, needing clear direction and resolve in finding my missing journal.

Still nowhere in sight, I tried to savor the moment at my clutter-free desk. Even though I had my Bible, devotionals and lukewarm tea, they were not comforting my nagging thoughts. Is my personal journal lost? Just then, my husband called on his lunch break. I proceeded to lament my dilemma to him; he suggested perhaps it could have slid underneath the car's back seat...just like his Bible had done on Sunday. After we finished our conversion, I headed to the car, hoping his suspicions would be correct.

Amidst the heavy down pour, I trudged to our van in the driveway. While leaning into the side, cold raindrops doused my lower back where my sweater and pants separated at the waist. Spurring me to purposely lean in further, sure enough, my precious journal was right where my husband had suspected. "FINDING YOUR JOY" displayed boldly on its cover, making me chuckle at its very appropriate title. Usually the front cover is hidden, bent back with the journal pages open and ready to pour my heart onto.

Immediately my mind thought about joy the way James chapter 1:2-4 AMPC describes it:

Consider it wholly joyful, my brethren, whenever you are enveloped in or encounter trials of any sort or fall into various temptations. Be assured and understand that the trial and proving of your faith bring out endurance and steadfastness and patience. But let endurance and steadfastness and patience have full play and do a thorough work, so that you may be people perfectly and fully developed lacking in nothing.

My idea of joy is not always God's idea of finding joy. It's more than a flashy, splash of joy written on a shiny white mug, making everything go as planned. Rather, it's about being joyful even when your joy mug seems empty and your plans have gone awry. Happiness is based on circumstances, while JOY is found in the Lord at any moment. True joy is experienced and known in our hearts regardless of what our errant notions of it are. Ever so slowly I'm learning the difference, experiencing joy that comes from the Lord and not my happenings. Finding joy when circumstances waver from my picture-perfect scenario, trusting in a God whose way is best.

But the fruit of the (Holy Spirit) (the work which His presence within accomplishes) is love, joy (gladness), peace, patience (an even temper, forbearance), kindness, goodness (benevolence), faithfulness, Gentleness (meekness, humility), self-control (self-restraint, continence). Against such things there is no law (that can bring a charge). —Galatians 5:22-23 AMPC

"Deep, contended joy comes from a place of complete security and confidence (in God) - even in the midst of trial." —Charles Swindoll

Prayer:
Thank you, Jesus. Your Word promises us everlasting joy and gladness shall be upon our heads. Fresh, abounding, overflowing joy from you, our strength and place of refuge. Holy Spirit, may our lives be ripe with Your love and peace, filling our cup with a continual supply of joy spilling over. Which, by the way, sounds like my cup of tea!

Confessions of a Too-Tight Tutu

Excitement filled the fall air as my first ballet class at the coveted Judy Marsh School of dance had arrived. At the mere tender age of eight, I felt well on my way to becoming a budding Prima ballerina. Thoughts had long danced in my mind, laced with ballet shoe ribbons, twirling images of lavish costumes and billowing tutus.

And now entering my class, I was full of anticipation accompanied by jittery nerves. Newly purchased pink tights provided the necessary support to my now wobbly knees. Little ballerinas, all in a flurry, energetically removed our coats and shoes. Emerging ready to dance, we donned soft, pink, leather ballet shoes, scurrying to position ourselves at the polished wooden ballet barre lining the mirror. Miss Marsh's serene voice instructed and encouraged her little ballerinas to greatness.

Each week I was resolved to faithfully attend class, while at home committed to practicing my newly learned dance steps. As the weeks progressed, my enthusiasm digressed with each class technique I could not master. What I had envisioned for myself and what I was capable of doing were two completely different things. From my perspective, it seemed so effortless, yet it was considerably harder and more difficult to perform. My spirits drooped right along with my now stretched-out tights.

My slouching deposition heightening after each class when I returned to a car filled with the wafting smell of delicious Fryer Tuck spuds. If only I had skipped class and eaten those tender morsels right along with my waiting mom and brother. Questioning yet again if class was worth missing out on the piping-hot bounty of potato wedges, I dug into the foil bag for a few lukewarm leftovers. This ballerina was swiftly losing passion and appeared on all accounts to be ready for her final swan song. Longing for warm spuds overpowered the lukewarm ballerina skills (or lack thereof).

Finding myself ready to prepare for the final curtain call on my short-lived aspirations, a second wind arose upon learning Mrs. Marsh had a Christmas surprise for us. Gathering at the ballet barre, anxiously wiggling and chatting, one by one we had our waists measured for her plans. Within a few short moments it was time for the golden measuring tape to be slipped around my waist. Completely confident of the proper etiquette when having one's waist measured, I did what I thought was the right thing to do...take a deep breath and suck it all in!

However, this "right" answer turned out to be terribly "wrong" considering I was getting fit for a tutu made with a snap closure waistband. Elastic would have been far more forgiving for a girl who loved Fryer Tuck spuds so dearly.

Immediately upon wearing this heavenly white tutu of layered tulle with a satin waistband, it exploded off my unrestricted waist every time I bowed to plie or simply just breathe normally. The class erupted in wild giggles as I instantly became the unintentional class clown, my cheeks warm from the blush of embarrassment. The dream of being a refined, elegant ballerina was already fading fast, and now it was gone in a "snap" because of my too-tight tutu. The time to lay to rest the dream of learning ballet had come, so I chose to retire this tutu and shoes into a box of memories.

Many years have passed since that final curtain call, and still somehow those memories seem rather unfinished. Thus, I began to trust in a God who loves to restore what the locusts have eaten. Deciding in my late twenties to give ballet a good ol' college try regardless of my mediocre skills...I signed up at Mt Hood Community College.

Mustering up the nerve to face my fears and attempt to relearn ballet, Once again I found myself in the same predicament...never finishing this class either. However, God who is so loving and full of mercy brought me needed healing, gently reminding me it's all about the journey and never about the envisioned or perceived destination. For not only did this class bring me more closure to my first wildly "unsnapped" ballet ending, it also gave me the idea of starting a cottage business making ballerina bears...which, by the way, is a whole other story!

Do you ever feel like you don't measure up? Perhaps you've had to "suck it up" to fit in. God's Word lovingly encourages us in Galatians 5:26 MSG "...not to compare ourselves with each other as if one of us was better and the another worse. We have far more interesting things to do with our lives, each of us is an original." Though I was too young to know then what I'm journeying to fully grasp now, my heart is profoundly grateful to God.

By His grace I am what I am, and His grace towards me was not in vain. —1 Corinthians 15:10 NKJV

And so it is with you. Because you matter to Him, more than trying to measure up in His eyes, as He beckons you to breathe freely and generously. His heart bursts with love and acceptance for the one-of-a-kind you. So, come into His presence fully accepting all He longs to give you, arms open wide to embrace you...too-tight tutu and all. You might possibly say to yourself, "Oh, snap! Why didn't I do this sooner?"

"Don't let people discourage you...just fluff out your tutu and dance away." —Author Unknown

You did it: you changed wild lament into whirling dance; You ripped off my black mourning band and decked me with wildflowers. I'm about to burst with song; I can't keep quiet about you. God, my God, I can't thank you enough. —Psalm 30:11 MSG

Prayer:
Precious Savior, I praise you for removing my black mourning band of lost loved ones, lost dreams or opportunities. Your Word says joy comes in the morning, so there will be a day when heavy mourning will erupt into whirling dance and lively song—a dawn of a new day. All praise and glory belongs to You for Your marvelous healing.

Dancing Queen

Strolling through the household items while at the Salvation Army store, my eyes were drawn to a beautiful picture frame. It had black, glossy details on crisp, white ceramic with a swirl of chartreuse, its top bedecked with a stunning jeweled crown. Upon examining the framework more closely, it revealed the beautiful scrolled words "Dancing Queen" written on the base. Thus far, this little gem was scoring winning marks on all counts...then, suddenly it plummeted from its number-one position.

How could I, a bona fide two-time ballet school dropout who preferred clinging to the ballet barre rather than venture out onto the dance floor, possibly relate to the declaration of "Dancing Queen"? Not an affirming message I hoped to add to my newly decorated craft room. When decorating, I find it important that items match the color palate or theme. Even more advantageous is if it holds a special meaning or memory that stirs my heart in such a way, making me confident it will make our house more like home.

Even though its title threw me off momentarily, this item was compelling enough to keep a hold of it, pondering it as an option. Continuing leisurely, I made my way through other favorite sections of the store while music softly played. Suddenly, I heard something that made my ears perk up. To my utter astonishment, the song from Abba called "Dancing Queen" started playing. Temporarily frozen in my tracks, clutching a frame bearing the very same title, I somehow gathered my senses. My legs began to propel onward looking for my family, excitement mounting while eager to show them this not-so-silly coincidence. It's what I call *divine hugs* from God.

No other sign was needed; this $2.99 purchase had a special meaning for me! What glory would it unfold as it graced my new space (formerly our oldest son's room)? Perhaps its presence reminded me to see myself in a new light; a light that had, through time, grown dim. Those childhood dreams of being a ballerina met with low confidence, skill and determination to be one. Plagued with self-depreciation in the mirror of my mind, this frame revealed a distorted image, even if it was a faint one. Over and over I rehearsed the lies and half-truths till they spun out of control; lies that I was uncoordinated and lacking self-discipline.

This little frame had already begun igniting truths to see myself with unlimited possibility. Dancing, if not fully in body (though I still give it a try in private), could certainly allow my spirit to confidently move within my soul, an open invitation graciously extended to all His sons and daughters.

Our King of Kings and Lord of Lords, who rejoices over us with singing, lovingly calls us to dance with Him. He moves us with glided steps, twirling freedom and leaps of faith producing joy before our feet even touch the floor. Eyes fixed on the lover of our soul, we never long to stray nor wander from His plans and purposes, staying in step with His lead. He remains completely enthralled with us, regardless of our two left feet, so captured by His acceptance with reckless abandonment.

What a comfort to know that this dance school dropout is free from the shame of past mistakes and labels imprinted with lies. The safety of the ballet barre is no longer needed beyond its true intent and purpose.

Clinging to Christ alone and letting go of our crutches, may "we throw open our doors to God and discover at the same moment that he has already thrown open his doors to us. We find ourselves standing where we always hoped we might stand–out in the wide-open spaces of God's grace and glory, standing tall and shouting our praise" (Romans 5:2-4 MSG).

When you do, don't be surprised to experience what Abba sings so poignantly—you can dance, and you'll have the time of your life!

Prayer:
Today, may you accept His invitation to dance. Walk away from past hindrance or good intentions and step out into your life filled with a plethora of dreams—a gleaming new start pulsating with vibrant hope. That can truly only come from the Lord.

Molehills Out of Mountains

Time was well overdue to remove the molehills that popped up in our front yard nestling up against the curb. The desire to spruce up our flower beds before spring was now joined with increased pressure to rescue my early blooming crocuses now smothered in mole mania. This pesky critter burrowing upward caused the crocuses' delicate foliage to croak under the mountain of fresh tillage.

Rather hating to admit it, I was ever so slightly admiring this particular mole's astute sense of focus. Managing to erupt orderly mounds in perfect rows while tunneling through our sod, somehow he was also able to keenly and systematically dot neighboring property with the same impeccable streamline mastery. Though I marveled that he was a gentleman of order, the mounding piles of dirt were still a blight on our lawn. It had been suggested by a friend that this was the work of more than one mole; if this was indeed the case, their impressive teamwork scored a virtuoso 10. Whatever the scenario, it was nothing short of a stellar performance.

Earlier, I momentarily reveled in their beauty when the heaps of soil were graced with a light dusting of snow. These works of art resembled a miniature Rocky Mountain range along our curb. It seemed to be a rare occasion to acceptably make a snow-covered mountain out of a molehill.

Shortly after removing the mounds of dirt, I felt joy and relief, hoping they had blazed a trail off into the sunset. As you can tell by what you have read already, I'm nowhere near being mole savvy—by far, I lack the full knowledge of what these little critters are capable of doing. Let's just say I greatly underestimated my opponent, and this startling truth became painfully evident as I gazed upon my recent edged and weeded walkway. Gasping at what my eyes were beholding...it was a fresh knoll of dirt burying my crocuses yet again!

Highly disappointed that my one little patch of orderliness was no longer in order, wrestling an all too familiar lie that tidiness should magically stay tidy—at least 24 hours, right? And when you cross it off your to-do list it should stay done. By now you'd think that after 21 years of being a stay-at-home mom and homeschooling our two boys, this elephant-sized fib would be debunked. Surely, I should have gotten that all too important memo. The truth is, in my heart of hearts I know the 411. Life is messy. Our 100% guaranteed "do overs" are things like dishes, laundry and other assortment of daily chores.

A slow learner by nature, it was regretfully being revealed yet again by my increased anxiety over this disheveled patch of a nearly perfect garden utopia. When such emotional intensity flies into my radar it warrants further examination as to why I'm experiencing the growing tension.

Recently, I decided to discuss this dilemma with my dear friend over lunch. She patiently listened as I dined away on my firecracker chicken, hoping to grasp the truth of my underlying issue far better than my novice maneuvering of chopsticks. My spirit was hopeful, because when we seek God, we find Him and the truth is revealed. As my friend and I continued our conversation, we were grateful for His faithfulness. I'm sure He was thoroughly delighted to mingle in with our laughter, tickled as we pondered Him, not distressed one bit at my raw emotions. I'm so grateful for the God-given gift of authentic, deep, spirited friendships.

At that moment I caught a glorious revelation that pulled me out of my "tunnel vision" (fitting for a mole). Once again, God spoke His truth over a well-worn path of misconceptions.

Like the mole's reappearance, two of my irksome Achilles heels flared up...one heel with a throbbing need for perfection, and the other aching with the distortion of *destination rather than journey* mentality. So rapid to appear, my spirit became disquieted, my thoughts distorted and routed for dissatisfaction instead of paths of peace that surpass all understanding. All of this because I chose to make mountains out of meager molehills.

I love what Zechariah 4:7 AMPC says:

> *For who are you, O great mountain (of human obstacles)? Before Zerubbabel you shall become a plain (a mere (a) (molehill)! And he shall bring forth the finishing gable stone (of the new temple) with loud shouting of the people, crying, Grace, grace to it!*

God makes a molehill out of our mountains. Oh, how I long to trust Him with mine.

Verse 6 of Zechariah 4 says how we can achieve this:

> *Not by might, nor by power, but by My Spirit*
> *(of Whom the oil is a symbol), says the Lord of hosts.*

So, until I get the problematic mole(s) eradicated for good, I will choose to let those mounds of earth remind me that God's turning my mountains of troubles into mere molehills. His grace is sufficient. This comforts my heart that I'm loved without performing or arriving; I can simply be His daughter, and the same holds true for everyone.

Do you have a looming mountain of human obstacles in your way? May we move forward in God's power and might, declaring His promise together, saying, "So, big mountain, who do you think you are? You're nothing but a molehill!"

"Shame loves perfectionists – it's so easy to keep us quiet."
—Brene Brown

Your life is a journey you must travel with a deep consciousness of God. It cost God plenty to get you out of that dead-end, empty-headed life you grew up in. —1 Peter 1:18-21 MSG

Prayer:
Jesus, You are truth and light. May You teach us to number our days and apply our hearts to wisdom. Only You are perfect in all Your ways. We long to walk in Your truth with peace and joy in our hearts.

Justice Like Snowflakes

The weatherman's predictions for a winter storm arrived as promised, delivering a healthy accumulation of snow. Before that, the season had only graced us with rapidly melting flakes and a scant light dusting of powder. Perhaps Mother Nature had grown weary of being poked fun at for her lackluster display of wintery splendor or was merely saving her best for last. Whatever the reason, it arrived that day blanketing our neighborhood with a soft hush that silenced the clamor. A glistening brilliant white coverlet stretched as far as the eye could see.

Snow has a way of bringing out the child within, beckoning us to come out and play. Reminiscing about my childhood, snow days were counted as some of my favorites. My brother and I raced to get bundled up quickly, braving the cold, enthusiastic to chuck freshly made snowballs at each other. Or we'd simply relish falling backward into a pile of snow, imprinting heavenly angels. Rounding out our day of fun was building an impressive snowman together.

As the years passed, occasionally our age difference caused a natural chasm of joint activities. One particular evening as twilight was settling,

I constructed Frosty alone. Street lights cast a glow and gentle flakes fell on my creation, but I was growing increasingly eager to remove my damp clothes and wrap my hands around a warm mug of cocoa. Crossing my cold fingers, I hoped we had whip creme or marshmallows to garnish my steaming drink.

Toasty and settled in, it was time to peer out the second-story window to admire my work below. Gazing downward expecting to be greeted by a beaming face, carrot nose and smile made of small stones, instead, to my dismay, someone had destroyed Frosty, leaving him in a heap. Anger and hurt welled up as I lamented my woes to my folks. Dad wasted no time to rise to this newly appointed challenge. Legendary in the neighborhood for chasing after anyone who messed with his property, no doubt he found this to be another golden opportunity to catch the culprits and bring them to swift justice. Fashioning a snowman for his trap, he carefully slipped into our darkened garage which became his makeshift stake out. Willing to wait patiently, the orange glow of his lit cigarette was the only clue to his whereabouts.

Not long after, two boys appeared, kicking this decoy snowman to its demise. They suddenly became aware of my dad's trap, his notorious reputation, and stellar gazelle moves, and ran away pell-mell! Before Mom and I knew it, my dad had not only caught the mischievous boys, but marched them back to the scene of the crime, instructing them to rebuild my demolished snowman...not to their liking or specifications no less, but to mine. Sharp contrasting scenes played out through the same window; one moment destruction, the next, restoration. Victim, to victorious! Redemption rolled out under my dad's watchful eye, and my soul warmed to the depths where the bitter chill of injustice once lay. God's Word tells us in Psalm 68:14 LB, "God scattered their enemies like snowflakes melting in the forests of Zalmon."

What a comfort to know God's got our back; He is mindful of every hurt and loss we have or will ever encounter. He watches over us like a protective Papa Daddy, comforting us with this promise:

"Anyone who strikes you strikes what is most precious to me." So the Lord Almighty sent me with this message for the nations that had plundered his people. —Zechariah 2:8 GNT

Even though I don't know what is going on in your life, I'm confident of this: God is a God of justice and He sends the neighbor bullies running. Your rejection, false accusation, harsh sting of injustice, or loss will be warmed with the promise of His love and faithfulness to you now and forever. Whether you see justice here or in eternity, God will work out all things for the good. All things plundered are tethered to His promise.

So, baby, it might be cold outside and even inside your soul too, but no matter the situation, allow God's sympathetic embrace to melt away any bitterly cold concerns and bring sunshine to your inmost being. His 100% emotional weather forecast is always accurate!

"When God is about to bless you, He first reveals your enemies."
—Author Unknown

Prayer:
Lord, cold winds of adversity and loss are always met with Your warm love and comfort. You chase the neighborhoods that taunt Your children to bring redemption to the weak and brokenhearted. We thank You for Your justice and strong arm of protection against our enemies.

Redemption from Perfection

While slowly packing the last remnant of 2013's Christmas decorations, I found myself reflecting on that year's Christmas. Pondering comes second nature to me, so my thoughts drifting into a bay of comparing it with years gone by was familiar waters. I asked myself this rather weighty and significant question: "In the last year, have I witnessed any areas of spiritual or personal growth?" Indeed, that Christmas was a paradigm shift, driven robustly by agents of change ushering in hints of transformation. Deep recesses of my heart needed greater redemption—perfection's futile pursuit being one of them. To the outside observer these appear as gentle whispers of change with the slightest of nuances. However, these subtle shifts have become glorious music to my ears, a symphony composed of clanging keys; Christ eagerly longs to free me from every cumbersome and binding shackle. This liberating sound is available to all who request it. The prophet Isaiah wrote of this very truth:

...He has sent me to bind up and heal the brokenhearted, to proclaim liberty to the [physical and spiritual] captives and the opening of the prison and of the eyes to those who are bound.
—Isaiah 61:1-2 AMPC

Liberty shows up in the strangest places. Recalling 2013's freshly acquired freedom, I surrendered my hopes for the "perfect" family Christmas card photo. Christmas 2007 heralds as the epitome; an unveiling of this revelation. As I gathered the reluctant family for a DIY portrait session that year, I recalled how it played out. For starters, we accidentally positioned the tripod smack dab under the bird feeder. Birds swooped wildly for seed, while the boys taunted each other mercilessly on the porch steps. Even after the bird feeder was repositioned to accommodate the hungry birds, our photo ops were fleeting faster than bird seed. We were rapidly growing weary of saying cheese and my sneaking suspicion told me there might not be a "perfect" Christmas photo to send that year. The small window to get a family photo had closed.

Fortunately, all hope was not lost. Our computer savvy son Derek offered to Photoshop the picture. Like magic he replaced a smile on his brother's face, painted his dad's white socks black, and made it all cohesive, changing the color to black and white. This photo still holds a special place in my heart knowing all the behind-the-scenes truth to get it that way.

Yes, 2013 was the year grief knocked the stuffing out of perfectionism and kicked detailed planning clean out of me, birthing the impromptu family Christmas photo on Thanksgiving day. A new season without my mom and recent family divisions fueled a desire to connect with my husband and children like never before. It did not matter if we had color coordinating outfits nor a winning Kodak smile. Kneeling in front of our six-foot Charlie Brown Christmas tree, we had each other. Sharing a common ground of loss and our own imperfections, by the grace of God we chose to rejoice in the midst of it all. The camera captured our real life—authentic and raw images never to see the stroke of Photoshop tweaking. Somehow it was perfect in all its imperfections.

Yes, that year brought growth and new-found freedom, timeless truth propelling me to even grander heights in the days ahead; deeper, more profound healing is headed my way. Now, that's truly something to smile about.

He will wipe away every tear from their eyes, and death shall be no more, neither shall there be mourning, nor crying, nor pain anymore, for the former things have passed away. —Revelation 21:4 ESV

"Perfectionism is the voice of the oppressor."
—Anne Lamott

Prayer:
Thank you, Father, for Your promised redemption from unhealthy perfection. Help us to see ourselves as beautiful diamonds, fully faceted by Your love. Hearing You speak boldly of who we are in You...we are already perfect in Your eyes.

The Letter

One day in 1986, it suddenly dawned on me: I wanted Kevin to move out of the "friend zone" into the "dating zone" ASAP! Only, I was hoping he felt the same way. The eyes of my heart soon opened to this new realization after he paid me a visit at Foxmoor clothing store where I worked as the manager.

Unbeknownst to us, our first meeting in the basement of Laurel Park Bible Chapel in 1983 would one day become life changing. Our sweet encouraging friendship blossomed in the soil of our personal brokenness. We sporadically touched base during the next few years, with occasional phone calls and hand written letters, even though we lived a mere three miles apart.

This gem of a soul mate was hidden in plain view during our friendship. Blinded by heartbreak of a short-lived first marriage, I plummeted head long into an eating disorder, my futile attempt to gain a measure of control in my life. There, in the midst of the pain and brokenness, God had a plan: to bring beauty out of ashes, oil of joy for mourning and a garment of praise for the spirit of heaviness.

Within a couple of weeks of Kevin's pivotal visit we waved good bye to the friend zone. Now standing hand in hand at the threshold of a new beginning, we eagerly awaited God's leading. Excitement sparked our faith, and faith moved us toward what the future would hold for us. We became increasingly aware that we had an adversary who was not ready to see us walk in victory. A persistent, seven-year battle raged within Kevin that unless he had total freedom from it, our relationship could not proceed to a commitment of marriage. My heart was not only longing to be married to Kevin, it was longing to see a tormented man set free. Faith rose within me to stand in the gap on his behalf and believe that God would deliver Kevin once and for all.

On one particular day, I felt the Lord's strong pressing to write Kevin a letter filled with God's truth of His deep love for him and mine as well. These truths were the keys that opened up the prison cell keeping Kevin in mental, emotional and spiritual torment and set him forever free from his particular battle.

Almost 37 years later, I still marvel at this beautiful tapestry woven with threads of God's faithfulness, grace and redemption. Whenever God's love is coupled with loving safe relationships, it never fails to bring healing. I'm eternally grateful for the love of God and committed relationships that loved me into wholeness. My life has forever changed for the better because of it.

Here are some excerpts from that letter.

> "Kevin, Honey, I pray with all my heart that the Holy Spirit will allow you to see the truth in God's powerful words and truths that have stood the test of time and struggle. Therefore, if any man be in Christ Jesus, he is a new creature. Old things are passed away, behold all things become new. God is never the author of bondage, wickedness or any other area of darkness. There is no bondage of darkness that Jesus Christ cannot break. This terrible bondage cannot be broken with good confession or good intentions; it cannot be broken with willpower. Only when we fully accept the great sacrifice paid at the cross, the blood of Christ breaks every bondage of darkness. Therefore, we can be totally confident of deliverance—set free by the power of His shed blood. Pray in the blood of Jesus; He will set you free. Remember this, it is truly the answer you have been searching for.
> Love you always, Lisa"

My letter was simply God's truths handwritten with love and faith, eager to see Kevin's transformation into a life of freedom. We have a God who is smitten with us, loves us through all eternity and died to set us free! May His resurrection serge life into you, bring you peace and joy unspeakable.

A dovetail of freedom unfolded from this match made in Heaven: I helped Kevin out of the black hole and to see God as His BFF, then he, in turn, has helped me learn how to trust healthy people. It's given me vital connections that have blessed my live so richly.

So if the Son sets you free, you are truly free. —John 8:36 NLT

"If you believe on the Lord Jesus Christ you are free."
—Dwight L. Moody

Prayer:
Lover of our soul, You are the one who sets us free. We are truly free by the power of Your blood and all You did on the rugged cross. You stooped down to make us great, by Your blood and by Your love. We bow down before You in humble gratitude.

Standing on Holy Ground

Whenever I hear the phrase "you are standing on holy ground," two thoughts pop into my head. My first thought conjures up the sacred soil encompassing the deep-seated roots of the bush that burned without consumption. This anomaly drawing Moses was immersed in unanswered questions far beyond a bush unyielding to the roaring blaze; it was a loving God desiring to capture His son's attention. His heart yearned to share the secret of a long-awaited deliverance, while reminding Moses His intimate knowledge of every injustice and crushing blow dealt by his enemies. Unknowingly, these promises were to be fulfilled. God beckoned Moses to loosen his dusty sandals in order to stand in His holy presence of destiny.

Secondly, when I'm not thinking about Moses, my heart is stirred to sing the beautiful worship song by Bill and Gloria Gaither, "Holy Ground." We can stand in His presence on holy ground just like Moses did.

Lately, I have been looking at holy ground in a whole new way. The Lord brought this to my attention when I stood on the grass of my childhood home one cold December. It was the second time I was near this house as an adult. In July 2013, my friends Kelli and Cynthia were kind enough to indulge me on my first birthday without my mama. A trip to my childhood home took precedence over visiting her gravesite; it was too painful, too fresh since her passing away two months earlier. I feared I would throw myself prostrate on her grave and weep. The weight and pressure of trying to keep it all together when she was alive was slowly lifting, yet I found myself not quite ready to experience her final resting place, especially on my birthday. Instead, we opted to visit my old neighborhood in Woodstock, Oregon, to take photos of familiar stomping grounds, including the now outside fenced yard of my childhood home.

There we were, three giggling ladies peering over the current owner's fence. This no doubt stirred curiosity, for it brought out Susan, the current owner, who was inside. She was gracious as we introduced ourselves and explained the reason for the obsession with her home. She happily shared information on the various neighbors I grew up with, while in turn I offered to make some copies of old photos of the home when we lived there.

In December 2014, I did an impromptu visit to Susan with newly copied old photos of the house—my home growing up—honoring my promise. I found myself swinging open the gate of my childhood home, feeling an overwhelming sense I was standing on holy ground. Endearing memories of the activities my family and I had shared there flooded my mind; memories like sitting by my brother Troy as we watched the crackling fire my dad tended to on the front corner of our lawn. Or the time when a car crashed into my brother's bedroom; as unbelievable as it sounds, he remained sound asleep amongst blaring headlights and broken glass.

Though there are countless more to share, I will end with one that makes me laugh every time it comes to mind. During one particular blustery winter, my mom bundled me up so tightly I could barely move. Basically my mommy made me into a mummy! Realizing what her zeal to keep me warm had done, she commissioned my brother to assist me if I happened to fall and couldn't get up. He became my own personal "Life Alert" system.

Precious memories were flashing before my eyes in the midst of my loss. Holy ground became an equilibrium where past and present mingled with pain and destiny. The great I AM who is the same yesterday, today and forever, comforts the afflictions of His daughter while promising a new beginning.

I'm not sure where life has you today, however, I do know whether you are in the lowest valley or on the highest mountain top God is your deliverer. You, my friend, are standing on holy ground.

"Life is the external text, the burning bush by the edge of the path from which God speaks." –Jose Ortega Gasset

Then he said, "Do not come near; take your sandals off your feet, for the place on which you are standing is holy ground."
–Exodus 3:5 ESV

Prayer:
Lord, we come into Your presence—holy ground undone by Your radiant glory and grace. We stand in awe of You and all Your wonders; Your abounding love and faithfulness reaches the highest high and lowest low. You, oh Lord, hold it all together and You are holding me right now.

Oh, Snap

"Oh no you didn't," rolled off my tongue with frustration as I tried to peer out our ice-encrusted windows. Mother Nature's cold snap was well into her third week of stellar performances. Gone was my initial happy dance at the first snowfall. Now, the lather, rinse, repeat of snow and ice made me want to wash this storm right out of my hair. Columbia Gorge's intense weather patterns only added to these unsolicited encores, producing vigorous storms for no extra charge. Yet it still cost those who faced its tempest; its super-size portions of snow, ice, and gale winds.

That day I found myself weary of this continuing storm; my spirits drooped much like the ice-laden trees buckling from the sheer weight. Desiring to be stout in spirit, capable to forge through this chilly adversity, I was hoping to counter the hand dealt to me with a sunshiny *Pollyanna* perspective. Instead, my cheery outlook was covered by a foreboding nimbostratus cloud. No way would you be hearing me belt out that I wanted the storm to rage on. The cold *did* bother me. What was Elsa thinking? And though the storm's fury paled in comparison to the poor folks I watched suffer on the nightly news, this storm was enough to wear me down.

As I looked to thaw my frigid faith, I grabbed my Bible, deciding to turn to Job 38. Right off the bat the first verse grabbed my attention. It read, "Then the Lord spoke to Job out of the storm." Could it be God was trying to get my attention with this long screeching halt, this intrusion to my day-to-day schedule?

Just maybe He wanted me to be still and enjoy the stillness of the winter wonderland—falling down into glistening snow's brisk arms to make an angel out of its powdery wonder, allowing my eyes to gaze towards Heaven's expanse. Or maybe cocooned in an ice castle with the King of Kings and Lord of Lords as His snow princess. Whatever the physical or spiritual climate, we are to be present in the moment not waiting for the storms to pass, choosing to dance in the rain (or snow for that matter).

Further on, God asks Job this question in Job 38:22 AMPC: "Have you entered the treasuries of the snow? Or have you seen the treasures of hail?"

Whenever personal storm clouds of disappointment brew, cabin fever of restlessness and irritability overrides my desire to seek the hidden treasures of the snow. Not to mention treasures can be hard to find when storms assail, buried in deep snowdrifts of heartbreak, grief, illness or other blizzards of loss. My snow-blinded faith can make it impossible to see God's bigger picture of provision and purpose. Many times, life's treasures lay concealed until we let our cold hearts slowly thaw from grief and disappointment.

Arctic blasts of doubt and fear blocked out God's warming presence from fully reaching my anguished soul. God never left me; it was only I who had lost my way.

It reminds me how, as a child, I lost my warm knit glove while walking home from school one snowy day. Arriving home, I sadly told my mom what had happened; with a sense of hope in her voice she said, "Let's keep this one in case the other one shows up."

Eventually, the snow melted and winter gave way to spring...my little glove now a distant memory. Cherry blossom trees lined the sidewalk as my friend and I intermittently skipped and giggled our way home. Stopping to catch my breath, my eyes suddenly spotted my little glove pushed up against a cyclone fence, nestled among a bed of dry furled leaves. Hope reborn, as lost is found, a treasure laid bare from melted snow.

God lovingly waits for us to partner with Him, syncing up to His truths, knowing in our "knower" His plans for us are for our good and not evil.

Those little gloves remain a beautiful reminder of that lost things can be still be found...even when we have lost our faith! It's just like Habakkuk the prophet complaints in Habakkuk chapter 1:1-3 ESV:

O LORD, how long shall I cry for help, and you will not hear? Or cry to you "Violence!" and you will not save? Why do you make me see iniquity, and why do you idly look at wrong?

Eugene H. Peterson (pastor and the creator of the Message Bible) has an introduction to Habakkuk saying this: "Habakkuk started out exactly where we started out with our puzzled complaints and God accusations, but he didn't stay there. He ended up in a world, along with us, where every detail in our lives of love for God is worked into something good."

Like Habakkuk, I no longer want to have my faith wheels stuck in drifts of *why* questions. Rather, I want to have the traction of trust produce forward movement as "I lean my entire human personality on Him in absolute trust and confidence in His power, wisdom and goodness..." (Colossians 1:4 AMPC my paraphrase).

God invites us to build a snowman, gathering splendid treasures from His majesty. Each unique snowflake of life experiences is rolled up and fashioned into something new, bringing a smile to our face from a jolly new creation—a gift wrapped up in His loving sovereignty. All of this patted down and molded with childlike faith gloves.

So, my friend, do you want to build a snowman?

"Winter forms our character and brings out our best." -Tom Allen

I thank you most High God! You are breathtaking.
—Psalm 139:5 MSG

Purge me with hyssop, and I shall be clean; wash me, and I shall be whiter than snow. —Psalm 51:7 ESV

Prayer:
God of all seasons, You are the maker of Heaven and earth. The heavens declare the glory of the Lord on full display for all creation to see. You find that which is lost and bring hope back to that which was once was buried. Your eye is on the sparrow, and You watch over each one of your children to bless and do good all the days of their lives.

An Angel Gets Her Wings

The first time I met Sharon was through my mentor friend, Lynn. Lynn was hoping to gather a few women for a Bible study she wanted to lead, and I was all for it. Right off the bat, my thoughts toward Sharon were she was as sweet as could be, soft spoken, gentle as a dove and altogether delightful. Her demeanor was such that you felt you had entertained an angel and doing so quite aware. Our small collected group of ladies soon began gathering for our weekly Bible time, leaning into God's Word to heal our hearts and share our stories.

One day, Sharon tenderly shared a story that has stood out to me to this day years later, still in awe of this glorious picture of God's transforming love.

You see, there was a time when gentle and demure Sharon would wear a necklace that had a tiny bell hanging ever so delicate from its chain. Since bells make noise that could bother her coworker in the next cubicle, Sharon politely stuffed the small bell with tissue to stop the clapper from doing what it was created to do: hit the inside of the bell to make it ring

Quite simply, she ceased its back-and-forth movement to muffle the sound that was meant to *be heard.*

To me, that bell became a clever representation of us three timid ladies who came together for Lynn's Bible study. Being led and encouraged out of timidity, we wanted to not only find God's love more completely, wholly and intimately, but our true God-given identity which would free up our voices in the process.

Somewhere along the way, that bell, like our lives, seemed better if it did not make the sound it was designed to. Perhaps that sound, those ideas or thoughts might upset people, make them uncomfortable or even worse...they may not like us. Some had even been told it was better to be seen and not heard, so with all those lies... we stuffed emotional tissue of self-preservation to cushion our fear of man, of being heard, drawing attention to ourselves or for that nagging clang of disapproval which seemed not worth the risk to...

Live out loud
Live boldly
Be free
Be Holy Spirit led
Live without restrictions or limitations

With all that being said, somewhere in our hearts we still carried within us a tiny bell of hope. That little bell was a stepping stone to truth, now temporarily buried in a lie. We longed for truth uncovered, lies eradicated and for our hearts to blossom fully into all the fullness God had for us. Grabbing a hold of God's promises and living 2 Timothy 1:7 AMPC out loud and unapologetically was all of our hearts' cries.

> *For God did not give us a spirit of timidity (of cowardice, of craven and cringing and fawning fear), but (He has given us a spirit) of power and of love and of a calm and well-balanced mind and discipline and self-control.*

Oxford dictionary describes the following words:

Craven: *contemptibly lacking in courage, cowardly, fearful.*
Cringing: *to feel very embarrassed and uncomfortable about*

something. To move back and/or away from someone because you are afraid.

Fawning: *to try to please somebody by praising them or paying too much attention.*

Those traits are things I simply do not want in my life ever. We are called to ring the bell of freedom loud and clear, silencing the blaring lies of the enemy once and for all for ourselves and others.

I love how bells beautifully symbolize beginnings and endings (see www.ire.minnstate.edu). Even the sound of bells from Aaron's robe were heard as he entered the Holy Place before the Lord and when he came out (see Exodus 28:35).

With Sharon's story, bells rang in a new beginning for her overcoming fear of man and public opinion, while learning the joy letting her voice be heard. Once and for all, every lie that once held her back was ended, and she no longer has issues with stuffing tissues (emotional or paper) to keep quiet. She is still sweet as can be and oh so angelic. I dare say even more so now, for she's living completely in her God-given purpose. Someone once said, "Sharon needs to be sharing more." I could not agree more.

Sharon's freedom had her ditch her tiny tissue stuffed bell and trade it for (the humorous thing some people say) more cowbell!

That, my friend, is what I call a true liberty bell.

Wise instruction are graceful garlands for your head and pendants for your neck. —Proverbs 1:9 my paraphrase

"Every time a bell rings an angel gets their wings."
—*It's a Wonderful Life*

"I got a fever and the only prescription is more cowbell."
—Christopher Walken

Prayer:
Lord, may we long to enter that Holy Place of time well spent with You. Thank you that You have got our coming and our going from this day forward and forevermore. Thank you that You love to hear our voice. Our voice is like music to Your ears. May we continually worship You and not be silent.

God's Grace for Every Season

 Winter

Jesus Christ is the same yesterday and today and forever.
—Hebrews 13:8 NIV

"Winter what good is the warmth of summer, without the cold of winter to give its sweetness." —John Steinbeck

Pocket Full of Promises

What has the Lord been showing you in this winter season?

_____

_____

_____

_____

Write a one-word take away to describe this season.

_____

For as the rain and the snow come down from heaven, and do not return there without watering the earth and making it bear and sprout and furnishing seed to the sower and bread to the eater; so is my word that goes out from my mouth:
It will not return to me empty, but will accomplish what I desire and achieve the purpose for which I sent it. —Isaiah 55:10 NIV

I'm single-minded in pursuit of you; don't let me miss the road signs you've posted. I've banked your promises in the vault of my heart so I won't sin myself bankrupt. Be blessed, GOD; train me in your ways of wise living... —Psalm 119:9-16 MSG

"Someone said that God gave us a memory so that we might have roses in December." —Sir Jim Barrie

Spring

"The deep roots never doubt spring will come."
—Marty Rubin

Some Bunny Loves You

Growing up, one of my all-time favorite places to shop was a bargain department store called Newberry's. My mom and I would venture to their downtown Portland location, which was always a special treat for me. This particular Easter season was no exception. Adding to all the excitement was my newly acquired spending money, which was burning a hole in my pocket rivaling the size of Texas.

Upon arrival, knowing the toy department was downstairs, off I went, nearly flying down the stairs with wings of joy, soaring to complete my high-spirited mission! Then, in the blink of an eye, there I stood—ever so slowly contemplating all the choices my budget would allow. Would it be a new outfit for my Barbie doll or a playhouse broom? Oh, the possibilities! Then, I saw them...third aisle, the lower right-hand corner of the shelf, piled high and overflowing from the wire bins. Amazing stuffed yellow bunnies, fluffy, adorable and cute as could be called to me.

Kneeling down, I gazed upon their faces as if to ask them which one wanted to go home with me. My first encounter with a jaunty Mr. Bunny happened, and boy he knew how to work it. His sweet demure made me 100% convinced he would make a lovely addition to my already charming collection of stuffed animals. Showing my mom this final decision, she looked at Mr. Bunny, and an inquisitive look came across her face. "Are you sure you want this one? He has a mark between his ears." "Yes!" I said with great conviction. I was sure it was love at first sight. My decision was a carefully chosen one; Mr. Bunny was the one, and I loved him, marks and all.

This can't help but remind me of the following precious verse in Ephesians 1:4 AMPC:

Even as (in His Love) He chose us actually picked us out for himself as His own in Christ before the foundation of the world, that we should be holy consecrated and set apart for Him and blameless in His sight even above reproach, before Him in Love.

God chose you! He looked down from His heavenly home and said, "That's the one I want; it matters not that it has a stain. I'm purchasing it with My blood, willingly given when I died on the cross. That sin-stained person belongs to me!" John 15:16 tells us we have not chosen Christ, but he has chosen us. What a comforting thought to be selected by a merciful God even with all our flaws. Through His gentleness and condescension, He has made us great. There's a part of me that wishes I would have saved Mr. Bunny in the keepsakes of my childhood memorabilia. He would have been a gentle reminder of how God chooses us no matter what. We don't need to have it all together to be loved by God.

In childhood innocence, I understood that love is not picking the best or the flawless, but purely loving without conditions. Jesus knows this about children, for He says for such is the Kingdom of God.

May we regain our childlike faith, a faith that is filled with wide eyed wonderment, in a God that has handpicked us, and who bought us with price...a price that only He could pay, to be part of His charming Kingdom. Now that is a Deal no one can beat!

This is how God showed his love for us: God sent his only Son into the world so we might live through him. —1 John 4:9 MSG

"You don't need to be perfect to be loved by a perfect God."
—Author Unknown

"Who being loved is poor?" —Oscar Wilde

Prayer:
Heavenly Father, thank you for Your unconditional love and forgiveness that flows freely from Your throne room. How can we ever thank You for all You've done for us? Your death on the cross brought us life; Your blood flowing from Calvary removed the stain of our sin and guilt. And we were purchased out of the bargain basement of darkness into the Kingdom of your glorious light. Thank you for adopting us and placing us in a body of winsome believers where I feel right at home...amen.

Redefining True Beauty and Brawn

There is no doubt in my mind that a good portion of my life has been strongly following what our society has focused on, whether it be outward appearances, position, or possessions, my fragile self-worth hinging vicariously on the approval of others. Compelling images on screen or print drove me to strive for acceptance as it encourages the population to worship physical beauty, strength and the dew of youth. Even though I know Proverbs 31 tells us, "beauty is vain (because it is not lasting...," still my past choices gave too much energy and exertion on achieving shiny bouncing hair, pearly white teeth or the "perfect" pant size.

Nearly 40 years ago it caused me to fall headlong into a crippling eating disorder after my failed first marriage. The grip of anorexia squeezed out any of the vibrant life God had for me, only being able to overcome its strong clutches through the power of my praying mother. Within a year, my eyes were opened to the devastation of what the eating disorder was doing to my body. Sadly, a few years later my poor body image reared its ugly head again due to my weight gain shortly after I got remarried. This time, I narrowly escaped a potential battle with bulimia. My husband somehow opened the bathroom door that I "knew" I had locked, and he saw me leaning over the toilet, about to rid myself of my last meal. This was a profound wake-up call from a gracious God sparing me from another pit of personal destruction. After that miraculous encounter, I never again struggled with any kind of eating disorder.

For the most part, I believe we can agree there is nothing wrong with admiring external beauty or brawn, enjoying healthy hair, whiter teeth or battling the bugle. Our bodies are the temple of the Lord, and we are encouraged to take care of them. As I age (hopefully gracefully), I want to shift my attention to a broader picture of true beauty and brawn—that which is not always highlighted in fashion or physical fitness magazines. I'm becoming more confident that true beauty comes from within and strength is measured beyond bulging muscles and washboard abs. Longing to view mankind as God does, I know His Word says, "Man looks to the outward appearances while God looks at the heart." It's not wise to judge a book by its cover as the prophet Samuel did when on a mission to choose the next king of Israel. Had it not been for the Spirit of God telling him otherwise, Samuel would have anointed the wrong man. He almost overlooked the ruddy David who tended sheep but had a heart for God. Once again God reveals that true "strength" and "beauty" has nothing to do with outward appearances, but rather what's in the heart and spirit of a man or woman.

God applauds the stouthearted spirit of the elderly, the perseverance of the disabled and all those battling crippling diseases or limitations, whether in mind or body. This reevaluation is pounding hard, hitting home as I watch a loved one's heroic stamina tackle life. Even walking, brushing their teeth, or eating has become laborious. This changes the face of what "powerful" really is—a rugged human spirit determined to live with dignity in spite of adversities. What I once put so much stock in has lost its value, challenging and rocking the very core of my flimsy standards. Smashing the idols of self-worth and worldly value, I'm realigning my perspective as to what real beauty and strength is.

The reality is, we all carry weaknesses, scars and flaws that reside in our hearts and minds, crippling us from soaring as God intended. A fortified internal city masks our shortcomings and inner wounds. And yet God beckons us through Paul's writing in 2 Corinthians 12:9 **AMP** to "glory in our weakness and infirmities, that the strength and power of Christ may rest (yes, may pitch a tent over and dwell upon me)."

For physical training is of some value, but godliness has value for all things, holding promise for both the present life and the life to come.
—1 Timothy 4:8 NIV

"To find the beauty within, look for the beauty in others."
—Author Unknown

"Anyone who keeps the ability to see beauty never grows old."
—Franz Kafka

Prayer:
Thank you, Lord, that Your love and approval does not depend on one's physical strength or outward beauty. In fact, true strength and beauty is determined by what is on the inside of a person. Not only that, but Your love is absolutely unconditional even in our brokenness. It redefines to a needy culture what true "beauty and brawn" is.

Welcome Change

While I was working with great toil to redo a garden area along the side of our house, my mind was a bevy of mixed emotions. This small area of land was my first attempt at gardening seventeen years prior, and I nestled it next to the detached garage of our starter home. Every year I would add an extra something to enhance its cottage charm—a climbing white rose, Lady's' Mantle from the annual Powell Valley plant sale, a blown glass snail, a precious birthday gift from my mama.

As our little slice of garden heaven evolved, so had our home; our starter home was now becoming our "finisher home." What once was a detached garage, became a very attached master bedroom. The new plans included a French door exit into a small enclosed patio adjacent to our bedroom. Hands laboring and feet planted firmly on the cold soil, I slowly began removing stones that lined our pea gravel path. Ecclesiastes 3:5 ESV came to mind as I worked: "A time to cast away stones and a time to gather stones." It was now the season to cast aside those familiar stones once gathered from a neighbor's yard, and then it began to hit me. It was more than just rocks, pea gravel and discounted plants dotting the small landscape. It had become part of this girl's sentimental journey. A discovery of beauty merging out of barrenness, kindred neighbors sharing their garden treasures.

Memories played in my mind with each new task of removing parts of my cherished established garden. As the day wore on, my feet became frozen and my heart was feeling heavy. It was then I decided to call it a day and head for a relaxing hot shower, hoping my body and soul would once again feel the warm anticipation of a new patio and not be laden with increasing sadness and the sense of loss brought on by change.

After placing my tools in the shed, I thought it would be nice to surprise my husband by cleaning up the dog's business, making one less thing to do when he got home. Who doesn't appreciate less poop to scoop, right? Grabbing a recycled plastic grocery bag, I quickly opened it and my eyes widened. Inside I spotted a fortune cookie paper. This was the only evidence from our delightful Kung Pao chicken we'd enjoyed weeks earlier. Placing one of my muddy garden gloves in the bag, I pulled it out and read the only two words that graced the slender white paper. There in small black type were the words "Welcome Change". These powerful words warmed my chilly soul. Leave it to God to show up in the most creative places, proving Himself to be faithful as He has promised, again and again, lest we forget.

Friends, are you facing change today? Perhaps not just small changes but big life changes? I know for me, my changes extend far beyond the borders of my tiny disrupted garden. Change at times can be an unwelcome guest forcing us to shift, transform and adapt to a new normal. With the Lord's unwavering help, I learned how to navigate my only sibling's diagnosis of early onset dementia, my mother's dementia and congestive heart failure. While adding into that mix, our first-born son left the nest into his newly purchased home, all the while being hormonally challenged! There were a whole lot of changes going on!

Whatever you are facing, you can be confident God has it covered. Join me in taking comfort in a God who does not change; He remains the same and never fails us. He is always faithful and pours out His everlasting love and mercy to us daily. His love will see you through every challenging situation.

You remain the same, and your years will never end.
—Psalm 102:27 NIV

For I am the Lord, I change not. — Malachi 3:6 KJV

"If you can't change it, change your attitude." —Maya Angelou

"Change the way you look at things and the things you look at change." —Wayne W. Dyer

Prayer:
Lord, thank you for Your unchanging love, where there is no variation, rising or setting or shadow cast by Your turning. Seasons change from springtime to harvest, but Your steadfast love remains the same. You, oh Lord, have appointed the moon for the seasons; the sun knows the exact time of its setting. From glory to glory You change us, while you are unwavering, timeless. Your truths transform us as we yield to Your perfect plan for our lives. Thank you for truth that sets us free.

Feathering the Empty Nest

It seems like only yesterday when Kevin and I filled the air with excitement as we delightfully prepared a room for the arrival of our first-born son. Fueled with anticipation and joy, we were more animated than the Daisy Kingdom wallpaper that paraded around the walls of his soon-to-be nursery. Light danced on the glossy white crib positioned beneath the window—each intricate spindle sanded and painted, a labor of love by my husband. The worn hand-me-down wood transformed into a crisp, brilliant white. The closet brimmed with an assortment of adorable clothes in a variety of styles and sizes for every season. A handmade wooden Noah's ark nestled in the far-left corner—my thrift store find just days after the thrilling news of "it's a boy!" was confirmed by the ultrasound imaging.

While waiting for Derek's birth, you could either find me waddling around (did I just admit that?), adding feathers to our nest, or propping my swollen feet up to read the latest how-to parenting book. As it drew nearer to the delivery date, so did my joy and optimism; confident my husband and I could do this thing called parenting.

Apparently there is no prerequisite to mastering this skill before you give birth to your first-born or even your second. For lo and behold, two-and-half years later, we welcomed our second son Trent. Doubling our happiness, his birth compounded the realization that books give you only limited training in the true art of being a parent.

Far too many mistakes later, we stand in awe at the honor of raising such wonderful sons in spite of our flaws and brokenness. Gloriously tallied into the raw equation is God's grace, equaling the sum that otherwise seems mathematically impossible.

Our babies once toddlers, tweens and teens, the day came when this stay-at-home mom and former homeschool teacher became an empty nester. No stranger to the knowledge of this incurring reality, it lingered in the far recesses of my mind since our boys entered this world. Aware of the fact that just as the appointed time led them to leave the womb, so also one day they would leave the nest.

A familiar quote by Reverend Henry Ward Beecher comes to mind: "There are two things we should give children, one is roots and the other one is wings." So, our baby just like his brother took flight, propelled by wings of independence gilded with freedom. Soaring to new exhilarating heights and rich depths, they are fulfilling all God has called them to be. Whether finding themselves atop mountains of successes or thrust down into canyons of failures, character and destiny still forge with every flap of their pinions.

Concluding that chapter in my life went all too quickly. After each son moved out, my heart waited for the dust of bittersweet memories to settle and the echo of an empty room to begin to pulse with life once again. Asking God's help transitioning into whatever He for me next, He re-feathers my nest with His promises.

I love Psalm 91:4 ESV's assuring truths:

He will cover you with his pinions, and under his wings you will find refuge; his faithfulness is a shield and buckler.

But those who wait for the Lord [who expect, look for, and hope in Him] shall change and renew their strength and power; they shall lift their wings and mount up [close to God] as eagles [mount up to the sun]; they shall run and not be weary, they shall walk and not faint or become tired. —Isaiah 40:31 AMPC

"Some people believe holding on and hanging in there are signs of great strength. However, there are times when it takes much more strength to know when to let go and then do it." —Ann Landers

Prayer:

Thank you, Lord, for Your faithfulness, a love that is never-failing and generous compassion, even mindful of every sparrow that falls to the ground. Your attention to the smallest detail brings a reassuring peace. We stand awestruck gazing at Your unfathomable love that comforts to the core and covers every human condition. We long to trust in You, Papa, grounded in the roots You have given us while we soar victoriously with You providing the wind beneath our wings.

Stretched by God

Two days are reserved each year to celebrate the birth of our two amazing sons. The months encompassing their births are heady with joyful memories and a good dose of warm fuzzies. Celebrating our firstborn son's birthday in March always calls to remembrance God's faithfulness on that glorious day in 1992.

Long before Derek was a twinkle in his daddy's eye, I prayed that God would bless us with a child, and just like all mothers do, I also asked that our child would be healthy too. Included in those petitions was a plea that my delivery would be speedy and absolutely no C-section. The diary of a wimpy woman right here folks! Though I longed to have a child, I was a chicken with a capital C.

Lo and behold, the day came when my home pregnancy test confirmed I was expecting; my joy knew no bounds. Each month as my tummy swelled, so did my earnest prayers. Not only was my appetite for food voraciously increasing, so was my reading of pregnancy books. This over-abundance of food tipped the scale, and the excess knowledge I gained from reading all about being pregnant caused a heavy weight of anticipation and anxiety as well.

When cheery daffodils rose from their winter slumber in spring, God's knitting of our son within my womb was complete. It was time to deliver the promise.

Portland Adventist Hospital was bustling with mothers to be in the maternity ward; apparently the stork was mighty busy that night! Throughout it all, I felt confident the Lord knew the plan I'd carefully laid out for Him. Once settled in, Kevin stayed bedside as visitors and staff came and went—while I tried to smile between contractions. So far, so good, until my ears heard a frighting statement from the nurse after checking on my progress. Pulling the sheet down, she said, "Oh honey, this baby is too big. I think you're going to need a C-section."

Crestfallen and gripped with fear my mind raced with the devastating news. She tried every trick in the book to comfort me, as did a dear friend moments later, bless their hearts. Nevertheless, I was completely panic stricken. I knew right then and there I needed my mama. Per my request, Kevin quickly stepped outside to go look for my mom and bring her to my room so she could pray for me while we waited to hear the doctor's assessment.

When I told my mama the news, she straightened up and confidently said, "We are not going to receive that." Planting her feet firmly on the ground, she boldly declared, "I'm going to stomp on that old devil." "Yes! Preach it, Mama," I thought to myself. The 12 hours of labor had me extremely tired and groggy. Mom continued to pray with conviction and determination. Monitors beeped and fear hung thick as she reminded God of His promises, quoting Scripture and interceding on my behalf. Zealously, she closed her supplication with, "Lord, stretch her like You stretched her dress."

One minute I was cruising on the freeway of agreeing prayer, then my reasoning hit the brakes. What on earth is she talking about? My weary mind was confused, unable to track her last statement. Quickly the Lord brought to mind the dress she referred to. It was a velvet Christmas dress I made one year earlier. After being cut out and shoulders stitched, it seemed from all appearances too small for me when I threw it over my head before sewing up the sides. Not needing my theme song to be "It's All About the Bass," I believing no amount of diet or exercise would get my bass to fit into that sewn up dress before my employer's Christmas party a mere week away. Desperate, I went to the fabric store and bought a yard of velvet to make two side panels. Words cannot begin to describe how unenthused I was with this last-ditch idea. "Side panels" sound a lot better for cars than a velvet dress. With that looming thought, I decided to forgo the panels and stitch up the sides anyway, hoping and praying it would fit. What did I have to lose besides the unrealistic idea of shedding pounds rapidly?

To my complete surprise it fit, and rather comfortably I might add. Now feeling like a princess in my homemade frock, I attended the delightful annual Christian Supply's Christmas Party, hosted that year at the beautiful Resort at the Mountain.

About that dreaded C-section, God answered Mom's prayer to stretch me just like He did my Christmas dress, eliminating the need to perform surgery much to the nurse's amazement. Oh, lest I forget, the one yard of fabric I choose not to use later became a little pair of velvet pants for Derek's first Christmas. God's perfect provision that was dearly needed for our already "stretched budget."

For you created my inmost being;
you knit me together in my mother's womb.
I praise you because I am fearfully and wonderfully made;
your works are wonderful, I know that full well.
—Psalm 139:13-14 NIV

"When God bends you He'll not break you. When God stretches you He'll not snap you. This is what the prophet Isaiah found out and if there was a prophet whom God stretched it was Isaiah." —Dennis Lee

A bruised reed He will not break, and smoking flax He will not quench. —Isaiah 42:3 NKJV

Prayer:
Thank you, precious Heavenly Father. You're so faithful to Your promises that are yes and amen. You hear our cries and hearts' desires as Your ear bends low to hear the faintest whispers of Your children. We rejoice in Your unfailing love that knows no bounds. We praise You for Your answer before we even see it.

We Are All God's Favorites

A shadow of favoritism formed over my mom at the birth of her younger sister, Donna. Her parents made the poor choice of comparing the two siblings throughout their lives...even on the most menial tasks. The sting of favoritism, coupled with comparison, delivered a deadly blow to my mom's self-worth. She was reminded daily of failure to measure up, and it haunted her long after her parents' passing.

Mom carried a distorted image God never intended her to gaze upon. She learned of God's love early on in life while sitting on a little bench in the basement of Minthorne Church's Sunday school class. But, her heart never fully recovered from the deeply embedded favoritism wounds that plagued her. Her tenacious love for God did enable her to overcome many hardships and disappointments she encountered along the way. And, God's love gave her wisdom and courage not to repeat the same mistake of showing favoritism and comparison towards my brother and me.

When we look at the definition of favoritism, it's "the unfair practice of treating some people better than others." This is contrary to God's nature. Numerous scriptures underline this intrinsic truth of His loving character. Romans 2:11 reminds us God shows no partiality and He is no respecter of persons. Peter exploded with this good news too when God revealed there was no distinction between Jew or Gentile. All are grafted into the same tree. He declares in Acts 10:34 MSG, "It's God's own truth; nothing could be plainer: God plays no favorites! It makes no difference who you are or where you are from. If you want God and are ready to do as he says, the door is open."

How freeing it is to belong to such a merciful and loving Papa who does not compare or measure, raise a high standard or base His love on conditions!

"God does not show favoritism..." —Galatians 2:6 NIV

"God loves you means You are God's favorite." —Grantley Morris

Prayer:
Dear Lord, I rejoice in a God who declares we are all His favorite. How comforting to know we are loved deeply, wholly and completely.

Published by *The Christian Journal,* May 2014, Lisa Jennings

Ladybugs Welcome

The sandy beaches of the Oregon Coast were a welcome sight. It seemed like an eternity since I'd last let the dissipating waves swirl around my toes and salty breezes brush my cheeks; in reality it had not even been a year. Hardship had crashed me against life's craggy shores and turned the tide of my emotional topography.

Just before my last attempt to grace the seaside, a dark storm loomed a day before our scheduled trip. My car accident left our van totaled and my body with whiplash and soft tissue damage. Instead of a trip to the beach, we made a trip to the Urgent Care.

This new detour map was dotted with treatments using a large portion of my energy toward wellness again. A mere 18 days after the accident, I received the dreaded phone call that my brother's battle with Lewy Body Dementia was coming to a close. Waiting for days as Troy hung on death's door, the hinges finally releasing him to Heaven's glory ten days later. I had to say goodbye to the most amazing brother one could ever have asked for. Even in his illness he walked with exemplary dignity and joy, touching lives wherever he went.

Waves of grief had been rolling in for years since his diagnosis, having to watch my mother and brother battle different forms of dementia simultaneously seemed unbearable at times.

And now, insurmountable waves of loss billowed over my soul as I watched my last family member be lowered into the earthen soil. Breakers of sorrow knocked my faith to the ground, leaving in its wake sadness and anger and littering my soul with debris of whys and confusion. Welling up in me was an anger towards God I was ashamed to admit. Who wants to acknowledge you're mad at God Almighty?. And yet in all honesty, we know He already knows. Psalm 139:4 makes it clear: "For there is not a word in my tongue still unuttered but, behold, O Lord, You know it altogether." He knows it and He loves us in spite of it! His Word reassures us over and over of His character. Psalm 103:8 NLT it tells us, "The Lord is compassionate and gracious, slow to anger and abounding in love." Or as the BSB translation puts it, He is "abounding in loving devotion."

He so longs to comfort us when we come clean with our wrong thinking. It is us who moves away, never the other way around. I love how the prophet Habakkuk questioned his tone toward God in Habakkuk 2:1 AMPC:

> *(OH, I know, I have been rash to talk out plainly this way to God!) I will (in my thinking) stand upon my post of observation and station myself on the tower or fortress, and will watch to see what He will say within me and what answer I will make (as His mouthpiece) to the perplexities of my complaint against Him.*

Habakkuk laid it out on the table of honesty, and God wasted no time serving him up a heaping portion of good news.

> *For... Then the Lord answered me and said,*
> *"Write the vision*
> *And engrave it plainly on (clay)tablets*
> *So that the one who reads it will run.*

*"For the vision is yet for the appointed (future) time
It hurries toward the goal (of fulfillment); it will not fail.
Even though it delays, wait (patiently) for it, Because it will certainly
come; it will not delay."*

God is working on our behalf to right the wrongs and forge positive changes in our lives. We then get to turn the tide, becoming a mouthpiece for His truth.

God has been gracious to me in all my kicking and screaming, quieting me with His love...and He started with a ladybug.

When we finally made it to the beach three months later, it was graced with tens of thousands of ladybugs on its glistening coastline. Sources have several explanations as to why these winged beauties gather at the water's edge. One theory is that after they have given birth, Santa Ana winds blow some to the coastal regions. How they got there I know not, but I do know my mission became to rescue as many as I could from the dirty foam and tide creeping up to whisk them away again. Delighted to scoop them up one by one into a small broken shell, I gently rinsed them with seawater if needed. Then, I allowed my arm to become a haven of rest to regroup, dry off, then poised themselves for takeoff.

My weary heart could relate to these small winged creatures. I, too, had felt stuck, weighted down and unable to soar. Helping them ultimately began to help me, reminding me of a verse in Zechariah 4:10 NLT: "Do not despise these small beginnings, for the Lord rejoices to see the work begin." How awesome is that? Whether we take big steps or baby steps, God is cheering us on! He also knows our necessities before we even ask. Most importantly, He loves to deliver us in our time of need. As I strolled to the beach with Kevin on that day of healing, my eye caught a garden sign that read, "Ladybugs Welcome". Yes, Lord, Your lesson from the ladybugs was welcome indeed.

Does anyone dare despise this day of small beginnings?
—Zechariah 4:10 MSG

"Even the tiniest things can be miracles." —Anonymous

"The ladybug wears no disguises. She is just what she advertises—a speckled spectacle of spring, a fashion statement on the wing, a miniature orange kite, a tiny dot-to-dot delight." —J. Patrick Lewis

Prayer:
Thank you, Papa Daddy, for being so gentle when we hurt, so patient when we linger in unforgiveness or anger. Your heart beats with nothing but love and compassion for Your hurting and lost children. Thank you for the gentle touches of grace swooping in to show love in the most precious and unexpected ways.

Grief's Persuasive Nudge

Grief's persuasive nudge finally got my attention. Oh, but I must tell you, my mind did a stellar job in subtle trickery convincing my broken heart that the grief work was already completed. Hands down, my flesh's preference leans toward maintaining the appearance of a neat, tidy package rather than over delving into a disheveled hot mess of emotions.

No twisting of the arm is needed when calling it quits on the whole grief process; quite frankly, it felt like a viable option. I was ready to vamoose, skedaddle, exit stage left and save myself from completely depleting my emotional bank account. Losing my only brother, Troy, to Lewy Body Dementia was not my first rodeo when it came to loss. A mere three and a half short years earlier, we said goodbye to our sweet mama.

Though I had made great intentional strides of grief recovery with my mom's passing, Troy's diagnoses overlapping mom's illness produced dark, permanent clouds of abiding sorrow. Barring a miracle, sooner than later I knew I'd walk through the valley of the shadow of death once more. When the dreaded news of Troy's rapid decline became a reality, my heart wanted to run away from the tsunami waves of sorrow, too weary to start the painful mourning process all over again. Resisting just like a swimmer's breaststroke push's away the water, I fought pushing away the grief after my brother's passing. Avoiding the boundary walls of necessary grief work, in a desperate attempt to regain a sense of normalcy I lost years ago. The core of my being longing to handle my grief in a healthy way, yet fighting the painful intrusion of this once again unwelcome guest.

The not so funny thing about grief is, you can run from it but you cannot hide from it, sooner or later that sleeping giant you tried to bury deep within will rear its ugly head. It's all part of God's beautiful design for our deeper healing and wholeness. He longs to equip us to face the Goliath of grief with our smooth stones of acknowledgment, permission and His strength. Bringing comfort to mend our fragile broken hearts, as He blesses us in the process. Fulfilling His promise written in Matthew 5:4 NIV "Blessed are those that mourn for they shall be comforted".

So how did God woo me into my needed grief work? By loving nudges as I watched various tender brother and sister interactions played out before me. Losing our beloved dog of 17 years little Buttony Boo. Leading me beside still waters as I slowed down my busy pace, gently redirecting my heart towards the pain and not away from it.

This thought came to mind as I swam one day, my body became tired of doing laps resting my head against the hard pools' edge I marveled at the pools utter stillness. After several minutes passed my legs wanted to kick again and do so with wild fervor holding the pools rough edge. Suddenly I witnessed the calm waters swift transformation. Watching this juxtapose an epiphany rose to the surface of my soul: "It was only when I stirred up the water in the turmoil of movement, that brought out the most brilliant color of blue rising up from the deep, Such depth of color was not revealed in the pools' stillness." My life longs for calm, smooth sailing without conflict. Jesus, however, called His disciples to a storm-tossed boat to show the depths of His faithfulness...

Roaring deep calls to roaring deep, life's upheavals, storms raging while Jesus sleeps. We cry out for calm, and it will come as Jesus declares, "Peace be still" over our battered souls. He lovingly invites us to yoke ourselves side by side with Him... "a man of sorrows," personally familiar with our raw anguishing emotions. He is more than able to handle the weight-bearing load of our sorrows onto His cross carrying shoulders. Bidding us to trust in Him through all our storms... encouraging us to give ourselves permission to grieve.

I love what Pam Vredevelt wrote in her book called *Empty Arms Journal*: "Healing requires us to stop traveling in five-speed overdrive and to turn down the noise. To move out of our heads and into our hearts. It may seem easier to deny, block, or repress our feelings, but denied feelings don't go away, they go underground, trapping us in grief."

Then she adds, "Opening your heart in the light of God's love, and acknowledging what is, is far more productive than resisting and denying the message of your heart. It empowers you to keep moving forward through your grief."

So, my friend, take God's hand in this journey called grief, opening your heart to His light, as He guides you every step of the way.

Wilderness and desert will sing joyously, the badlands will celebrate and flower ... Like the crocus in spring, bursting into blossom, a symphony of song and color. —Isaiah 35:1 MSG

They'll sing as they make their way home to Zion, unfading halos of joy encircling their heads. Welcomed home with gifts of joy and gladness as all sorrow and sighs scurry into the night.
—Isaiah 35:16 MSG

"You will lose someone you can't live without and your heart will be badly broken, and the bad news is that you never completely get over the loss of your beloved. But this is also the good news. They live forever in your broken heart that doesn't seal back up. And you come through. It's like having a broken leg that never heals perfectly that still hurts when the weather gets cold, but you learn to dance with the limp." —Anne Lamott

Prayer:
I thank you, Heavenly Father, for being my healer as I walk through grief. God of all comforts, I praise You for binding up my broken heart to allow deeper healing to take place.

Bye-Bye Pack Rat

Anyone who knows me well is privy to the fact I tend to collect things. I'm a self-proclaimed pack rat of doohickeys, whatchamacallits, sentimental mementos and all things shiny. Our attic is a land of misfit objects to provoke tender memories or some form of creativity.

Due to my tendencies toward over accumulation, shrinking attic space has become the end result; now bursting at the seams, it groans from over stuffing. It's like a waving banner capturing my attention to begin the journey of downsizing. Heck, even a pack rat's nature is to let go of certain found treasures to grab a hold of something new and more desirable.

I've noticed a correlation between deep physical housecleaning and emotional housecleaning. For me, they seem to go hand in hand. In times past when saying goodbye to these accumulated treasures, it usually reveals an unhealthy thought pattern that needs to go as well. Though the interweaving of the physical and emotional purging is key, the actual letting go process can be painful.

There is a bittersweet underlying tone that sets the mood for change. Change is hard even if it's for the better, especially since we are creatures of habit. Whenever my reliable apple cart gets upset, I tend to scramble to pick up my disrupted pile of apples...even the damaged ones. I scoop them up, carrying them close to my heart as I climb back onto my rickety cart of familiarity. The dichotomy of God's Kingdom runs interference with my unwholesome attachments and misguided thinking.

God loves us for who we are but too much to leave us that way. We no longer need to cling to the status quo or our tired, worn-out coping mechanisms. God says in Isaiah 43:18-19 GW,

> *Forget what happened in the past, and do not dwell on events from long ago I am going to do something new. It is already happening, don't you recognize it?*

I don't know about you, but I'm so ready to do some spring cleaning emotionally and physically! Traveling lighter by emptying my suitcase of fear, worry, doubt, unforgiveness, or anything crowding out Jesus' truth and goodness is best. Instead, I intentionally pack kindness, love, joy, laughter, and forgiveness. No longer am I traveling with my neck poised to look in the rearview mirror of yesterdays or what if's. Rather, I'm keeping my eye on the prize—His promises—as hope rises from the ashes of my past.

There are still doodads, whatnots and precious family memories tucked away in our attic—now a healthy balance of treasures. Today, this self-professed pack rat is more of a mouse. Through all the decluttering process, my personal growth is blossoming, saying goodbye to nonessentials to grab a hold of the essential. How refreshing!

Behold I am making all things new. —Revelation 21:5 ESV

"Every loss leaves a space that can be filled with God's presence."
—Amy Boucher Pye

Prayer:
Lord, we ask for a fresh new start, springing forward and bursting with Your visions, dreams and endless possibilities. May our minds and hearts de-clutter from anything that crowds out Your plans and purposes for our lives. Thank you for this promise in Your Word (2 Corinthians 5:17 ESV): "Therefore if anyone is in Christ, he is a new creation. The old has passed away; behold, the new has come!"

Honey from the Rock

My husband Kevin and I love hunting for agates. His love for finding agates grew when he lived in Newport, Oregon, for five years as a child. Mine did, too, while celebrating many of my July birthdays with my family at Agate Beach, which just so happens to be in Newport as well! We have often pondered if we saw each other as children, passing our future soulmate unaware.

To this day, rock hunting still brings us joy...and a little friendly competition whenever we search for these little treasures together. Positioning our heads down, our eyes have laser-like focus as we comb the beach's landscape. The oceans sights and sounds are a mere backdrop for the sole commitment to score the mother of all agates. From time to time, we break from our individual dedication to conquer this quest and pause to share our findings and marvel at each other's good eye and fortune. For as long as we've been married we've shared this fun activity, possessing plenty of agates to prove it.

Our annual agate hunt one year was unlike any other. On this particular weekend, we joined our dear friends Joe and Susy to celebrate their 43rd wedding anniversary at a hotel and beach area we'd never been to. Not only was it thrilling to commemorate their special occasion, experiencing a new beach sight was an added bonus.

The weather forecast looked bleak for our trip, with heavy rain and high winds predicted. Understandably, this gloomy prediction dampened our spirits, causing second thoughts to creep in. For me personally, not only was the weather looking stormy, so were my emotions. I was brooding, sad and in a funk—in dire need of a sunny deposition. Like our friend Jim says, "Going to the beach is like mental floss." Apparently, a good hardy flossing was in order. Thankfully we all pushed through those pesky apprehensions concerning the weather; committed to pressing on, we had an unwavering resolve to go, come heck or high water.

Though I unwillingly packed up my sorrow with me that day, God found a way to break through the sadness with a promise that weekend. After arriving, we had a delightful evening of fun, food and fellowship in spite of the rain.

By morning we were amazed; the rain had ceased and the skies were clear. Now I was chomping at the bit, eagerly wanting to walk on the beach. Kevin was tired and his back was hurting, so I made the trek down to the beach by myself. My prayer was, "God, please show Yourself. My heart is hurting; I need Your peace and comfort." In all honesty, I also prayed that He would lead me to find a glass float. Hey, it never hurts to ask!

Even though He never did reveal a shimmering glass orb, much to my delight He did expose a beautiful agate which I immediately bent down to pick up. It was a good size, and to my surprise, there were countless more of these little gems. Upon this great discovery, I wasted no time to call my husband. "You have to come down here...there are so many agates!" My persuasion was lackluster at best, and he lovingly declined my offer while waving to me from the motel's deck in the distance.

As I continued walking without my trusty agate buddy, I found even more agates, feeling sad Kevin was missing out on one of his favorite things to do. It became clear that drastic times called for drastic measures. So, with determination, I went back to the motel to prove the validity of my findings, confident this could possibly seal the deal. Reaching our room, I opened the door and laid my treasures on the ground near Kevin while he was on the floor rolling out his back. His interest peaked at my finds, realizing I indeed did hit the agate jackpot. Wrapping up his stretching, he was now ready and eager to join me in the hunt.

The exhilaration of faith becoming sight always brings a fresh wind of hope, a new found strength and a desire that rekindles our souls. How delightful it was to share the best agate hunting event ever with my partner in crime. I won't tell you who found the biggest agate that day. It's not nice to brag! But I will tell you this location is at the top of our list for a revisit.

While traveling home, I decided to read about how agates are formed in God's creation, and it is fascinating! One explanation was that they develop as secondary deposits in hollow cavities called "vesicles." The layers form in stages, and the cavities are irregularly and uniquely shaped.

Those little stones tell a story of beauty wrought by a gaping hole. This beach trip revealed a hole in my heart formed by brokenness. Feeling so cavernous through my lens of pain, it seemed almost impossible to heal. As I talked with the Lord on the beach that day, He had me stop and watch the people gathering treasures from the sea. Once storm tossed and battered, they were now a token of resilient beauty, being collected in joy and wonder. As I observed people stoop and gather the gems, God lovingly whispered in my spirit, "Someday, your pain, loss and heartbreak will be a nugget of hope and healing to those whose hearts are breaking." Instantly the pain lessened with the reminder His bigger picture is far grander than my eyes could see in my present state.

Your heart might feel emotionally split like a canyon of grief, undone by circumstances that took your breath away. Yet God knows it all; nothing slips through His loving fingers to defeat you. All His unending love and devotion to you will fill your gaping wounds with His glory. Honey comes from a rock, sweetness from extreme bitterness, hopelessness turns into resounding hope. Your heartache transforms into a memorial gem of sparkling redemption, bringing joy to other sojourners who long for the same freedom.

O you afflicted (city), storm-tossed and not comforted, behold, I will set your stones in fair colors [in antimony to enhance their brilliance] and lay your foundations with sapphires. And I will make your windows and pinnacles of (sparkling) agates or rubies, and your gates of [shining] carbuncles, and all your walls [of your enclosures] of precious stones. And all your [spiritual] children shall be disciples [taught by the Lord and obedient to His will), and great shall be the peace and undisturbed composure of your children.
—Isaiah 54:11-13 AMPC

But He would feed Israel with the best wheat. I would satisfy you with honey from the rock. —Psalm 81:16 HCSB

They will feast on the abundance of the seas, on the hidden treasure in the sands. —Deuteronomy 33:19 NIV

When you're between a rock and a hard place, it won't be a dead end. —Isaiah 43:2 MSG

"This is (a gate) to wonder." —Author unknown

Prayer:

Lord, we praise You for Your healing touch to broken hearts. Nothing is ever wasted in Your Kingdom plans for Your children. Thank you for helping me see earthly woes with heavenly wonder, soaring like a kite with a tail of Your unfailing love.

The Avenger

Having two boys and a husband who love action movies like Marvel films pretty much narrowed my chances of seeing a chick flick down to next to nil. Which, by the way, is absolutely fine with me. I thoroughly enjoyed being with them, having a shared experience and embracing the motto "If you can't beat them, join them." The movies were action packed and full of adventure—good vs evil, with good ultimately prevailing. But, hands down, being in the company of my family was impossible to beat!

Kevin and I occasionally carry on the tradition of an action-packed movie night. Presently, we have added a few chick flicks to our viewing selection. Possibly to your amazement, Kevin enjoys some of them as well. My husband, what a hero!

Speaking of heroes, Jesus our true conquering Hero paid the ultimate price on the cross for our sin and shame. His Word tells us in Isaiah 53:5-6 MSG, "He took the punishment, and that made us whole. Through His bruises we get healed. We're all like sheep who've wandered off and gotten lost. We've all done our own thing, gone our own way. And God has piled all our sins, everything we've done wrong, on Him." How refreshing, load lifting and brimming with hope this is; hope that never disappoints.

After going to see the *Avengers Endgame* movie, my morning devotion had me land on Jeremiah 51 in the Message Bible, which at the time seemed random. However, it did not take long to see why my choice was not random at all...but rather, quite divine. The words leaped off the page, grabbing my attention far greater than any adrenaline-driven movie moment. Right there in verses 34-37 was a thrilling, life-changing revelation: "Then I, God, step in and say, I'm on your side, taking up your cause, I'm your Avenger!" Wow, friends! How epic and reassuring—good triumphing over evil, hope cascading over despair, delivering a mighty blow to the enemies that loomed over us. All the while, He washes away injustices with a love that is undeniable. This tangible, palatable victory is far removed from the bad taste left in our mouths by guilt or embarrassment. This overcoming, conquering King is in our corner 24/7, never sleeping or slumbering...even when you cannot feel Him. That is truly an *Endgame* changer!

God pleads our case, rights our wrongs, restores what has been devoured, loves us so fiercely, and champions for our peace, salvation and joy. What is our role in this glorious package? Simply receive it free of charge; your admission has already been paid for. I've had the joy of seeing fresh areas of God's redemption in my life. One significant area involved spearheading a last-minute planning for my high school 40-year reunion. On a whim, and being my first rodeo in regards to planning a reunion, it sounded like fun. None of this could have been done without my two delightful sidekicks, Janet and Judi, who were gracious enough to come along for the wild ride.

To be truthful, I am surprised we were able to pull it off in the short amount time, not to mention the lackluster funds and potentially a low turnout. But we stayed on task amidst all our laughter and lively conversations during our planning sessions. One thing we were confident about, no matter how it played out on reunion night, we would have fun connecting with our classmates and each other.

Yet, through all the laughter, joy and encouragement these two brought, my heart had some trepidation beyond the normal reunion jitters one might experience. For my heart was carrying a dark secret—one I had only shared with a handful of people since it happened over 40 years ago. In my heart, I knew I needed to share what happened to me in the safety of their friendship. It was imperative so that I could continue my healing journey upward and into a place of greater freedom and victory. And in doing so, I was embraced with deep love and support from both of them. My apprehensions melted away and my heart was greatly comforted.

Now, moving ahead, though difficult, I feel it's important to share my story, not in a place of sorrow or victimhood, but of victory. I love Revelation 12:11 AMPC: "They have overcome (conquered) him by the means of the blood of the lamb and the utterance of their testimony..." So, in that truth, I can now share that I was raped during my senior year by a fellow student. For years I wrestled with shame, guilt and sorrow, trying to bury my trauma so I could face each day and pretend life was normal. Adding to the difficultly was never being able to tell my parents about being sexually assaulted, which left me feeling alone, and with no one standing in my corner defending me. Somewhere in the depths of my broken and shattered soul I felt responsible.

It took me years, with the Lord's help and love of others, to unpack the truth of that dreadful night...that it was never my fault—ever. Though that person apologized after the event, it was a long bumpy road before I arrived at true forgiveness. I've realized along the way, that in order for a person to be able to abuse another human in any way shape or form, is out of such brokenness that only God can truly heal them. I hope and pray he has found the freedom and peace God longs to give him.

God, in His unfailing love, has redeemed the areas of sexual abuse that go far beyond that one painful night in December of 1978 to a place of healing, peace and joy.

The night finally came for our 40-year class reunion. The turnout was great, and it was a night of joy and personal redemption, fully enjoying my classmates with such love and freedom. My 40 years of wandering in a high school wilderness of memories, now entered a promised land of fresh new beginnings and a satisfying do over. Just like the Joel 2:25-26 NIV promises:

I will repay you for the years the locusts have eaten—the great locust and the young locust, the other locusts and the locust swarm my great army that I sent among you. You will have plenty to eat, until you are full, and you will praise the name of the Lord your God, who has worked wonders for you; never again will my people be shamed.

"Not all heroes wear capes mine wore a crown of thorns." —Unknown

"We are not called to be superheroes, but to be heroic in a superior God." —Forthefamily.org

Prayer:
Lord, thank you for being our Avenger, taking up our cause with love while also desiring freedom for both sides involved in the heartache. We praise You that the pain of yesterday is swallowed up in the victory of today. We praise You that those who put their trust in You will not be put to shame or disappointed. You are by far the best superhero ever.

Live Your Life Joyfully

Losing my mom was difficult and though I had a little over a year knowing her inoperable blown heart value would take her life barring a miracle it's still hard to say goodbye.

I loved my mom and I knew she loved me, and with all that being said we had our relationship challenges. Some people would have called it codependent and I would have to agree. Many times my husband felt he was married to me and my mom. It was a vicious cycle my unhealthy patterns were unable to break for many years. I do believe it was never my mom's intention to do so however truth is wounded people wound people no matter how hard they try or don't want to. The beautiful redemption story is healed people heal people I love that precious promise that Jesus provides.

Though I had gained so much freedom with my mom I still had some sticking points. One was always worrying I would give my mom heart palpation's, she got when she was pregnant with me and continued throughout her life Many times if I went anywhere, especially on a trip, her worry would set off her heart to beat rapidly. I chose throughout my life to not do as much for fear of my mom getting sick.

So, one day as I pondered my mom's loss and sifting through the grief I heard the Lord say, "You have waited your whole life to live; now live your whole life." It was like a permission slip from God a hall pass to go where I wanted or needed without the guilt, or a foreboding fear of losing my mom.

I love Matthew 11:28-30 in the AMPC:

Come to Me, all you who labor and are heavy-laden and overburdened, and I will cause you to rest. (I will ease and relieve and refresh your souls). Take My yoke upon you and learn of Me, for I am gentle (meek) and humble (lowly) in heart, and you will find rest relief and ease and refreshment and recreation and blessed quiet) for your souls. For My yoke is wholesome (useful, good—not harsh, hard, sharp, or pressing, but comfortable, gracious, and pleasant), and My burden is light and easy to be borne.

So many times in our lives, we can be yoked to the wrong thing, even with the purest intention.

I wanted to protect my mom so she would not suffer, and yet I was hurting myself, my husband and even our children in the process. Yoked to Jesus is the best way to walk out our lives, for His Word promises us such joy and freedom.

So, with that permission slip from Jesus, we finally took a trip to Disney World with our grown sons and had a lovely time. My husband and I overcame a fear of flying (well, to a point), and I even used the suitcase my mom bought to go to Disney World with my brother and his family back in 1992. I share more of this amazing story in my Fall section called "Flying the Friendly Skies." God was so gracious on that lovely trip. His hand was in every detail, making it a truly magical vacation from start to finish.

"Cherish your yesterdays, dream your tomorrows and live your todays." —Anonymous

Prayer:
Jesus, Loving Father, how we worship You! You are the giver of life—abundant life. We thank you for the joy of being yoked to You, which brings nothing but good. Thank you that it's never too late for a happily ever after with You.

God's Grace for Every Season

 Spring

Let us know; let us press on to know the LORD; his going out is sure as the dawn; he will come to us as the showers, as the spring rains that water the earth. —Hosea 6:3 ESV

"Where flowers bloom, so does hope." —Lady Bird Johnson

Pocket full of Promises

What has the Lord been showing you in this spring season?

_____
_____
_____
_____

Write a one-word takeaway to describe this season.

_____

And they waited for me as for the rain, and they opened their mouths wide as for the spring rain. I smiled on them when they had no confidence, and their depression did not cast down the light of my countenance. —Job 29:23 AMPC

"If God had a refrigerator, your picture would be on it. If He had a wallet, your photo would be in it. He sends you flowers every spring and a sunrise every morning... Face it, friend. He is crazy about you!"
—Max Lucado

Summer

"Spring being a tough act to follow, God created June."
—Al Bernstein

Beauty in Barrenness

A while back, my husband and I watched Steve and Geoff the *Meteorite Men* trek through barren, high altitudes—parts of the Chilean Desert called the Imilac Strewnfields; as far as the eye could see, it looked lifeless to me. I'm not a big fan of the desert, however if you add an extra S to *desert*, it becomes the word *dessert,* which I *am* a huge fan of! I did become enthralled with the whole process, Seeing that void stretch of terra firma reminded me of my life at times.

When my spirit feels barren, arid and lifeless, the grit of my circumstance blurs my vision to no longer see any evidence of value or purpose in the wasteland of suffering. How comforting to know, even in our desert times of feeling spiritually dry and parched by life's scorching trials, God sees the value. The nuggets of truth, tried by the fire and ready to mine the deposits left by our painful feelings of loss and devastation. Steve and Geoff were excited with the possibilities...

they saw the gold mine that lay at their dusty boots, armed with magnetic devices and keen eyes they gushed at the wealth they were beholding, one precious rough rock at a time. So, too, God mines our souls, sweeping across them with the powerful attraction of His grace, stooping down to marvel at the beauty and value—which we often mistake as worthless. Beauty for ashes, life spoken over the dry bones, humanity formed from dust...God's redemption in the most drought-stricken and lifeless situations.

How precious to have such a loving Father—to see the value when we see none, to rejoice over what the world would overlook.

Matthew Henry |*Commentary* says, "Afflictions are among our mercies. They prove our faith and love, they humble our pride, they wean us from the world, and quicken our prayers."

Isaiah 43:19 MSG reminds us, "Forget about what's happened; don't keep going over old history. Be alert, be present. I'm about to do something brand-new. It's bursting out! Don't you see it? There it is! I'm making a road through the desert, rivers in the badlands."

"Let the thankful heart sweep through the day and as the magnet finds iron, so it will find, in every hour some heavenly blessing."
—Henry Ward Beecher

Prayer:
Heavenly Father and miner of our souls, thank you for knowing firsthand the value in suffering. As we travel through the desert, may Your well-traveled hand guide us with Your truths and water our weary and torrid souls. May our minds be refreshed in Your promises and the hope that one day we will be come out of the wilderness, leaning on our Beloved. Make us strong, fortified with Your walls of love, seeing beyond the pain to Your exceedingly bright and precious promises. Thus, knowing that You make all things work together for our good. From glory to glory, one priceless nugget at a time...

Divine Mocha

After much talk of getting together, Michelle and I finally nailed down an afternoon coffee date. Asking her to select the java destination from a plethora of local coffee shops, she suggested Divine Mocha. I was excited! This quaint little spot was once The Little Red Store, a market conveniently located a stone's throw off the side of the road. Years ago, this was the perfect place for my friends and I to stop and gather refreshments after a long, hot day of berry picking. This made me all the more eager to experience its transformation, reminiscing about the good old days while I sipped my cup of tea.

Before meeting with Michelle, I had planned to accompany our son Derek to his appointment with a Realtor. It was thrilling to think this house was a block away from us, precisely the same street my husband lived when we were dating. Pulling up to the vacant house to wait for the Realtor, Derek and I chatted about the home and other topics, occasionally glancing at the clock from time to time. Thirty minutes later we realized the Realtor was not going to make it. Derek and I parted ways so I could head down the road to meet my friend... processing the disappointment that my son's meeting never transpired.

Pulling my van into a parking space, I grabbed my purse and made my way inside the charming coffee shop by a creek. Michelle was already there, enthusiastically conversing with Barbara, the delightful Christian owner. By the sounds of it, the two knew each other well, adding to the already homey feel. Upon finishing our warm exchanges and introductions, I established myself up against the counter as rustic wooden planks creaked beneath my feet. Continuing to listen to their engaging conversation, while gazing at the menu, suddenly, my ears perked up to the words "short sale." As I listened more intentionally, I realized this woman not only sold coffee, she also sold homes. My vision now expanded more fully to see glossy Realtor business cards on the counter and her office right behind me. Joy flooded my heart as I became increasingly aware this was not only "Divine Mocha," it was a Divine Moment. God showed up amidst my swirls of doubt and disappointment, serving me a "Yes and Amen" to His promises. My faith stirred like the pools of Bethesda, realizing He answers prayer in the most unexpected places. Feeling caught off guard by His goodness, even though His proven track record of never failing or forsaking is impeccable. Clamoring at the sheer glory of it all my heart swelled, as God showed up with creative flair, His attention to detail, which usually involves rib ticking humor. Hello! He is the Creator of the universe. Luck and coincidence are not even worthy opponents to God's grand outpouring of blessing and favor. A simple commitment to meet a friend turned into the best visit to a coffee shop ever.

As I drove home, Barbara continued to run her cozy shop, pouring heavenly mocha's and making delicious sandwiches, while her son Tim who is also a Realtor, met with Derek to show him the home. Once again, a few short hours later, I found myself pulling into that same parking lot, this time to watch our son sign papers for his first home, in a coffee shop of all places!

Put your hope in the Lord. Travel steadily along his path. He will honor you by giving you the land. —Psalm 37:34 NLT

"Every divine appointment is preceded by a season of preparation. And if we submit to the preparation, God will fulfill His promise. If we don't, He won't. Why? Because God never sets us up to fail."
—Mark Batterson

Prayer:
Lord, what a difference a day can make or an hour or even one minute. Every now and then, we have the joy of seeing You move on our behalf in less than 24 hours. We rejoice in those rapid replies while we commit to learning to trust You more when we have to wait, knowing you make

all things beautiful in Your time. You are the God of suddenlies and moving slowly...whichever brings out the best in us. You care exceedingly more about our character than our comfort. Thank you that Your Word says, "This is the day that the Lord has made, I will rejoice and be glad in it." And that, my friend, is Divine.

Flotations of Faith

Do you ever feel that the demand on you is greater than the supply? Or perhaps you feel what you have to offer pales in comparison to what it takes to meet the need. Well, do I have good news for you! First of all, you're in good company. Moses, rescued from a basket floating in the Nile, grew up to see the unveiling of a promise that started swaddled in a blanket of his mother's love. Tenderly, she was nursing seeds of greatness and destiny. As Moses grew, he stood at the edge of that destiny scared, trembling at his weakness, lacking eloquence, not equipped to be a man of words, slow of speech, and having a heavy and awkward tongue.

Moses' heart burned like the God-fueled bush, fully ablaze with a fiery passion to serve. Yet flames dossed with the stark reality of his lack. Somehow, Moses must have thought God was unaware of his shortcomings. Perhaps pointing them out to God one by one would change the course that God was mapping out for him. God, however, did not allow how Moses felt about himself derail His divine plans for deliverance. He chose to send a deliverer; a deliverer who also needed delivering. Human fragility was imprinted with the image of Yahweh—equipped to do the work in his human condition.

Moses the mouthpiece was slow of speech, but had a mouth formed by Almighty God. As God was freeing His people from bondage, He was freeing Moses as well, His all-consuming fire burning the chaff, breaking inadequacies and chains. His truths would set Moses free. Honesty, I have lost count of the times I have told God of my lack. Sure, I know "I can do all things through Christ which strengthens me" by heart. God's Word is true, for He is not a man that He can lie. But still I find myself doubting or even comparing myself with others, knowing full well I'm not supposed to.

And when faced with an assignment that required shoes too big for my feet to fill, I look to God and want to say, "Are You talking to me?" Questioning the God of the cosmos, He's the one who knitted me in my mother's womb and knows me intimately. He knows my rising and my sitting, and He finds intrinsic value in each one of us.

As I write these words, I pray little by little, precept upon precept, line upon line I will grasp His truth—truth that will empower me. I long for the day I will no longer say, like Moses, "Here I am, Lord—send Aaron." For now, I will go, trusting in a God who knows all about me and loves me anyway. Me plus God equals mountain-moving faith, faith that my five loaves and two fish offering can feed the masses simply because God blessed it. Using me, this "basket case" of woven insecurities will reveal God's glorious case through a basket.

My presence will go with you, and I will give you rest.
—Exodus 33:14 ESV

"God can turn your biggest flaws into your biggest cause."
—Mandy Cane

Prayer:
Lord, bless our hearts with a burning desire to follow You and trust where you lead. May we know Your strength is made perfect in our weakness and glory in it, because where we are weak, You are strong. Thank you that the big shoes we may be called to fill can be removed as we stand on Your holy ground—where size does not matter. Thank you that we serve such an awe-inspiring God who sees our less as *more*.

Happy Feet

Typically, my morning ritual includes checking Facebook, scrolling for updates and recent posts. I'm sparked and awakened more fully by reading witty quotes, comments, or perhaps deep provoking thoughts to ponder. Since I'm not a coffee drinker, this invigorates my senses rather nicely, while also keeping me abreast of joys and possible challenges my family or friends might be encountering. Presented with opportunities to bless and receive blessings, I can share words of encouragement and offer prayers for one another.

However, on one particular morning I was not greeted with a warm inviting cup of Joe replacement. Instead, I was quite shaken by a cruel stinging attack which was written with malicious intent. Even though this relationship had broken down recently, how could this person, someone I've loved and supported for many years, want to tag me in a photo calling me a "liar, a cheat, and a scam"? Reality hit like a jolt of ice-cold water dousing my tender heart. From this new vantage point, my hope for redeeming love and mending the forlorn fence between us looked like it was the last thing on their mind.

Thankfully, before this rude awaking, I'd spent time in God's Word, reading Psalm 35:23-26 MSG. Pondering this scripture, I decided to call a friend to share these verses...they were simply too good to keep to myself!

"Please get up—wake up! Tend to my case. My God, my Lord—my life is on the line. Do what you think is right, God, my God, but don't make me pay for their good time. Don't let them say to themselves, 'Ha-ha, we got what we wanted.' Don't let them say, 'We've chewed him up and spit him out.' Let those who are being hilarious at my expense be made to look ridiculous. Make them wear donkey's ears; Pin them with the donkey's tail, who made themselves so high and mighty!"

Upon finishing, we both chuckled at how the Message Bible interpreted what King David wrote. My mind immediately flashed back to the Disney classic *Pinocchio* with its Pleasure Island's Amusement Park. This place promised fun to young lads, yet unbeknownst to them lay a hidden entrapment...a spell cast on all who dared to partake in this magical land. This mischievous entertainment would cost them their true identity, producing donkey ears and tails burgeoning up on naive boys—rather fitting for the wrong choices that Lampwick, Pinocchio, and all the other boys made, landing them in such a foolish predicament.

David knew firsthand what it felt like to be relentlessly pursued by his enemies—King Saul being his chief nemesis. David wrote throughout the Psalms his laments for God's justice and deliverance from Saul's unmerciful attacks. In Psalm 27:12-14 NIV he cries, "Do not turn me over to the desire of my foes, for false witnesses rise up against me, spouting malicious accusation."

He continues with his bold declaration in verse 13: "I remain confident of this: I will see the goodness of the LORD in the land of the living. Wait for the Lord; be strong and take heart and wait for the Lord."

We serve a God who sees it all: the cruelty, injustice, false accusations, and lies that have been waged against us. His truth will prevail, and your character will one day be restored. You might not see it today or the day after, but one glorious day you will see the goodness of the Lord on your behalf.

Our job in all this is to trust the Lord, ask forgiveness for any wrong doing we may have done, and forgive those who have hurt us. I don't know about you, but taking the high road in an offense is never easy. My flesh wrenches and craves to retaliate and seek justice...*now.* Although Jesus tells us to forgive someone 70 times 7, it is not a math equation I'm gleeful about. Yet, if left unsolved, it produces far more heartache. In the Sermon on the Mount in Matthew Chapter 5, Jesus taught His followers The Beatitudes, which encourages us to be glad in our persecution, happy even when people revile you and say all kinds of false evil things against you. Beatitudes is inherited from the Latin word *beatus*, meaning both happy and blessed (Vocabulary.com).

I confess...as the day lingered, I still did not find myself happily jumping up and down over this person's mean-spirited maneuver. Determined to not let them rob anymore of my joy, and choosing to take the high road in goofy merriment, I grabbed my high-top purple canvas sneakers with plaid trim...my combat boots of joy. Confident, I was sure they would put a smile on my face as I stepped into all God's reliable and trustworthy promises.

Are you facing one of life's zingers? May I encourage you in your movement forward with this hope from Ephesians 6:14 AMPC: "... shod your feet in preparation to face the enemy with firm footed stability the promptness, and the readiness, produced by the good news of the gospel of peace. Each new step bringing more freedom and victory." Hey, how about sporting some goofy shoes while doing it! I say if the happy shoes fit...wear them.

"Be sure you put your feet in the right place, then stand firm."
—Abraham Lincoln

Prayer:
Precious Lord and Savior, You see every wrong done to Your children, and Your heart breaks. You are a God of justice, mercy, and grace. Help us to say, as You did on the cross, "Father forgive them; for they know not what they are doing" (Luke 23:34 NIV). Lord Jesus, we put our trust into Your loving care.

Love Covers All

During the summer of 1965, my mom came to the realization she needed to overcome her fear of driving. Even though her driver's license found a secure home in her sleek wallet, anxiety prevented her from getting behind the wheel much. A stay-at-home mother of two, her desires to head out on the highway increased, taking us on adventures that went far beyond public transportation.

Only a mere four years old at the time, the thought of a new escapade was thrilling to me. I was positively eager to lend Mom encouragement, humor, or both to enhance her pending endeavors. I wasted no time fulfilling this assignment the first day she backed out of our driveway and ventured down rutty Tolman Street. Rather pleased with herself, we rolled up to the first stop sign in downtown Woodstock. Summer's balmy breeze tousled Mom's brunette curls through the open window, and I was tickled pink sitting behind her as my brother sat shot gun. Immediately, I noticed a uniformed sailor stepping off the curb to use the crosswalk. What a perfect opportunity to showcase my newly acquired skill of wolf whistling. Pursing my lips, I gave a hardy whistle, leaving my mom looking like the culprit and blushing profusely when she realized what I had just done.

Mom pressed through her fears and my antic to take the yellow Thunderbird out for more spins. Whether it was driving to Sears to purchase a plastic boat for my brother, my cousin, and I to float down the stream of Westmoreland Park or a picnic at Eagle Fern, she now had wheels coupled with a new-found confidence.

One day, after a long trek of summer fun, Mom was happy to be home and eager to park the sweet chariot in the garage. Lining up the car, she carefully began to proceed, when all of the sudden a loud crunch abruptly interrupted her typical parking protocol. Misjudging the distance, the car hit the right side of the house. Visibly shaken, she began to assess the damages while simultaneously fearing what my dad would say when he came home from work. Noticing my mom's behavior, I began to hatch a plan, which went as follows.

Right before my dad would arrive, I would first, position myself in front of the crash site. Second, fan my sundress over the location of the accident. And third, smile really big. Nothing unusual about this behavior says no one... No doubt my dad found this display extremely suspicious—and a rather odd way for his active daughter to spend a summer day.

My parents got a big chuckle out of it, and I'm guessing my wholehearted attempt to protect my mother defused some heated emotions that day.

God's Word talks about covering one another in 1 Peter 4:8 AMPC: "...above all things have intense and unfailing love for one another, for love covers a multitude of sins (forgives and disregards the offense of other.)"

When I think of "a covering," I think of the story of Noah in Genesis chapters 6 through 9. How thrilled Noah must have been when he was finally able to get off the overcrowded ark, to place his two feet on solid ground, breathing in refreshing air after his extended cruise with some smelly shipmates.

He began to cultivate the ground and planted a vineyard. All those days on the water made him long to get some earthen soil between his fingers. As a native Oregonian, I've seen a lot of rain in my lifetime, so in a small way I can relate to that.

Noah's vineyard yielded a bumper crop of grapes, so he made some wine and partook of it...to the point of becoming drunk, laying naked and uncovered in his tent. Shortly after, Ham, one of Noah's sons, glance at his father in his birthday suit and rushed to tell his two brothers outside the tent. Ham was ready to "ham it up" about his dad's nakedness with his two bro's, but Shem and Japheth would have no part of it. Rather, they took a garment, laid it upon their shoulders, walked backward so as to not see his nakedness, and covered him.

Choosing not to expose his vulnerable state, nor mock it, but out of respect, they covered it. How easy it would have been to have guffawed it up with Ham at their father's expense and weakness at the moment, instead of extending grace to him. When Noah awoke from his wine-induced sleep and found out his youngest son's poor behavior, he cursed him, but spoke blessings over Shem and Japheth.

Chances are, we've all, at one time or another, had someone expose us in our point of personal weaknesses or shame. Cruelty or a need to belittle to be big can drive some to attempt to capitalize on a weakness.

The Lord longs for us to be "Love Coverings," protecting the weak, broken, and vulnerable. God's Word says in Matthew 25:36 AMPC, "I was naked and you clothed me, I was sick and you visited me with help and ministering care." When we bless others, we not only bless the heart of God, *we* are blessed in the process. God is calling us to be a covering of forgiveness and grace. So, today may we spread SONshine of love coverings to those around us, then experience the SONshine of God's love and blessings shining down on us.

"A blessed life is led by grace." —Author Unknown

Prayer:
Thank you, Jesus, for Your tender mercies and loving kindness that blots out my transgressions. Lord, may we forgive others as You have so freely forgiven us. Grant us a blanket of grace to cover those who need it and a voice of truth in love when we need to confront. We all stand naked before You, Lord, exposed and broken. Thank you, Lord Jesus, for the heavenly attire of grace, mercy, compassion, and forgiveness You've clothed us with. May we stand as a people poised and ready to walk side by side, draping your children with the same.

Door Closed? Paint It!

A refreshing breeze brushed my cheeks as I lounged on our back porch in a comfy camping chair. Birds chirping joyously encircled around and about our property, harmoniously singing their cheerful praises amidst the dull hum of freeway noise in the distance.

Journal in hand, I was ready to pour out my heart to God and listen to what He had to say to me. "What do You want me to do, Lord?" I asked Him. This seems to be a frequent question I ask. Kids are grown, Mom is gone, brother's dementia is increasing, and unresolved conflict plagues my extended family. My world has drastically changed as I once knew it.

A few reoccurring questions bounced around during that time in my life. Do I go back to work after 22 years of not being part of the work force? Do I need to spend more time writing? What should I do with the extra time I have, Lord? I waited to hear some answers from God to my perplexing questions while my eyes soaked up the garden sights. The end of May into June never fails to unveil its fullness and beauty after winter's bleak hibernation. Purple and white Irises bloomed profusely around the glistening pond, and goldfish darted within. Pink roses climbed vigorously around our black, wrought iron arbor leading to our shed, perfectly framing our freshly painted door. I reveled in my relaxing vantage point.

Rather pleased with the new door color, I was eager to see how this "Surf Spray Blue" would one day compliment the "Woodlawn Sterling Blue" house color my husband and I had just agreed upon. Gazing at the door, thoughts floated into my mind like drifting clouds—one being how amazing it is that one little can of paint can make such a difference.

My next thought wandered to this quote: "When God closes a door, He opens a window." Through the years, I experienced mixed feelings about this quote I read on a wall plaque while working at Christian

Supply long ago. The Lord has spoken to me more than a time to two about my limited understanding regarding this quote. Truthfully, how invigorating is the thought of an open window, where light and fresh air transforms a space. On the flip side, a closed door can feel claustrophobic and confining.

My immature faith hinged on my limited perceptions of God. Now, years later and after many "closed doors" in my life, I see the blessing in not crossing thresholds I was never meant to. God's protective boundary lines are drawn in pleasant places, revealing His exceedingly great and precious promises. So, what do we do with a door that God closed? I say, let's paint it! Change the image and how we view it. With a brush stroke of thankfulness that it did not open, we cover it with a new coat of fresh perspective, producing a dynamic makeover for one's soul.

We can be consoled by the truth that God always closes doors for a reason. Sometimes we are privy to those reasons, and other times it remains a mystery. We know there is one door God always wants to remain open: the door to our hearts. Revelation 3:20 AMPC says, "Behold, I stand at the door and knock; if anyone hears *and* listens to *and* heeds My voice and opens the door, I will come in to him and will eat with him, and he (will eat) with Me." By far, this is the best "open door" you will ever know...

Open up, ancient gates! Open up, ancient doors, and let the King of glory enter. —Psalm 24:9 NLT

"I don't know how the door will open...but I know the hand that opens the door. —Hosanna Wing

Prayer:
Thank you, Jesus, You open up doors of freedom, opportunity, and hope. How we praise You for the doors You shut for our well-being,

fostering the greater good in our lives. Lord, we open up the doors of our hearts wide for You. Search our hearts, for only You hold the keys to total joy and fulfillment.

The Fruit of Redemption

When our son Derek was a child, he would occasionally ask me to plant an apple tree. While writing this, I'm wondering why I didn't fulfill his request and plant this fruit-bearing gem. Perhaps my reasons were lackadaisical or reluctant...sighting lack of funds, being too busy, or not being keen on having more trees than we already had, which now seem rather weak reasons for not giving in to his modest petition.

Though my wheels stayed stuck in indecisiveness back then, Derek's wheels spun with ingenuity, excitedly coming up with clever the idea of planting the seeds from his freshly polished-off apple. His small fingers removed the tiny seeds of hope from the exposed core. At the time, kneeling down beside him to dig a hole for the seeds felt like that would be good enough...mission accomplished!

Funny how reflective you can get when your kids grow up, as the woulda, coulda, shoulda, rapidly take root unlike those little apple seeds buried in the clay soil—which, by the way, never saw the light of day. Life, however, is full of "if onlys" that can easily sprout up, towering over us with preeminence, shading us from God's warming grace.

As I ponder my mothering skills in the pool of reflections, there were areas that sparkled where I loved deeply and selflessly, while other spots appeared murky, clouded amidst my human frailties and brokenness. Though I tried to do my best, I've shed some tears at those lost opportunities and have mourned my losses.

Stepping away from these reflections has given me the occasion to ask forgiveness where I have wronged my sons and husband, even the best intentions can, sadly, go awry or be sorely misunderstood. Words cannot express how profoundly grateful I am for forgiveness. God is the perfect example, and my husband and sons are a close second. God's Word promises those who have been forgiven much love much. I now love mucho grande! As sweet as forgiveness is, I believe restoration is the cherry on top. How can we not love resuscitating a do over? Breathing new life into a past mistake...a little slice of heaven I say!

My mind thinks of that every time I see my "redemption" Pixie Crunch Apple Tree I planted when Derek was 16. I made the purchased after reading the following description in the Henry Fields garden catalog: "a favorite apple with children because of its flavor and its ability to bear reliable annual crops the second season without the need for cross pollinating." I calculated that Derek would have fruit from his apple tree by the time he was 18, just under the wire of when most kids leave the "nest."

At the age of 16, his love for apple trees had been replaced with computers, drawing, and hanging out with friends. Now, I felt it was up to me to plant this pathetic-looking twig all by myself with high hopes this spiny branch would one day blossom and bear fruit of redemption.

To my surprise, that sad, barren twig brought forth fruit two years later as promised. Nearly bursting my buttons with pride, I gazed upon the fruit tree laden with its ripe, petite apples. With quickening steps, I joyfully made my way into the house informing Derek he could now pick the apples from the tree he'd always wanted. Ya, about that...it turns out he wanted an apple tree to *climb* in. Wow! Apparently I never got the memo! Somehow, not only did I miss the boat, I wasn't even near the shore!

It makes me laugh every time I think of it. Now, when I see those small, sweet apples weighing down their slender branches, I marvel at how good God is. Regardless of our flaws, good intentions, and attempted do overs, fruit is still capable of growing out of the soil of our mistakes. Thriving and flourishing, it's because of God's love and tender mercies—which is the best fruit of all.

Who is this coming up from the wilderness Leaning on her beloved?
Beneath the apple tree I awakened you...
—Song of Solomon 8:5 MSG

"Anyone can count the seeds in an apple, but only God can could the number of apples in a seed." —Robert Schuller

Prayer:
Lord, we echo the prayer of David in Psalm 17:8 NIV: "Keep me as the apple of your eye; hide me in the shadow of your wings." Thank you for doing that in season and out of season, in sweet success and bitter failures. Help us give ourselves permission to not stay weighed down with past regrets. Instead, let us choose to taste the sweet freedom of Your bountiful orchard of grace.

Tender Hearts and Thick Skins

Janet and I were neighbors and all-around best buddies—our closeness evident by a telltale photo of the matching outfits we sported on our grade-school field trip to OMSI (Oregon Museum of Science and Industry). We planned our wardrobe down to the lucky rabbit's foot dangling from our Levi belt loops. Really though, how lucky could that poor rabbit have been?

When I think of Janet, my mind is flooded with happy memories and funny stories; they are like brilliant stars nestled in a night sky of gratefulness. Janet was a treasured childhood friend to share silliness and secrets, whether walking to school, playing together, or during sleepovers, experiencing laughter till our sides hurt brought on by the countless goofy ways we could amuse ourselves.

One of our favorite games was playing Montgomery Ward's Catalog. In our day (which sounds incredibly old), you could pick up and return your orders to the Mall 205 Ward's store. Back then, they relied on employee customer service and good old fashioned handwritten files to keep track of it all. What fun it was to play after school, setting up shop downstairs on my parents' covered pool table. A toy pink phone for imaginary calls...check, a Ward's catalog...check, files made up with fake names like Frank Frone...check—all the proper tools to ignite our wild imaginations. Why we never worked at Montgomery Ward's when we got older I will never know. We had serious mad skills I tell you!

While in grade school, we chose to clean the handwritten graffiti from bathroom stalls during recess just for fun! Each school week was occasionally mingled with some mischief...at times, less than angelic. We'd round out our Fridays with belting our hit single: "We're going home today, today, today!" ushering in our weekend. It makes me giggle at the very thought of it.

One moment we walked to grade school as children, and next thing you know, we were catching the bus to junior high with the first stroke of blush applied to our cheeks. Time flew by, but the memories linger, remaining a steady source of joy.

So much so, while at a grocery store check stand recently, gazing at the outrageous tabloids that slander and exploit people, a childhood memory of Janet and I surfaced. I stood there wondering how someone being attacked handles such lies, falsehoods, and slander without being able to tell their side of the story? It's a two-sided coin only baring one, oblivious to the other side's details.

I'm pretty sure we've all struggled with hurtful and untrue stories told about us that slammed against the walls of our integrity, casting suspicion on the foundation we hold so dear. Sometimes, I'm guilty of setting my eyes on only one side being represented, believing that to be the whole truth without hearing the other side.

As I wrestle with my own personal pain from the untruthfulness spun against me, it presses me into seeking answers for the injustices. This question mumbled within me as I unloaded my shopping cart: "How do they do it, God?" I gently heard the words *thick skin* rise up in My spirit along with the memories of how Janet and I had a pre-summer ritual.

Before each summer arrived, we would prepare our tender feet for the freedom of barefoot days by toughening them up. Our solution: a "foot boot camp" without boots. These tender feet, previously cradled in warm socks and comfortable shoes and barely seeing the light of day, would be exposed to the sunlight, dark, hard asphalt, and rough cement—going "all natural." This quickly acclimated our tender soles to lessen the nuisance of feeling every poke and jab of the harsh ground beneath. Thus, our ritual gave way to a foot-loose and fancy-free summer!

It made so much sense to me back then, and it's so applicable to me now. My tender heart and thin skin feels every poke and jab of harshness and disapproval of others toward me, focusing my attention on my wounded soul. Instead, I want to use these opportunities to develop a thick skin of grace, foregoing their deep potential wounds. This allows me the freedom to enjoy the green pastures the Lord leads me to or even the rough harsh asphalt—His endless glory stretched out beneath my eager feet regardless of circumstances. His glowing canopy of approval and forgiveness gives me the strength to go on.

As for you, you meant evil against me, but God meant it for good...
—Genesis 50:20 ESV

"Cherish all your happy moments. They make a fine cushion
for old age." —Christopher Morley

Prayer:
Lord Jesus, thank you so much that we're able to throw open our doors to You and discover, at that same moment, You've already thrown open Your door to us. We find ourselves standing where we always hoped we might stand—out in the wide-open spaces of God's grace and glory, standing tall and shouting our praises (Romans 5:1-2 MSG) with our tender hearts and thick skins encircled more fully in Your love.

She Flies With Her Own Wings

"Alis Volat Propriis" is the Latin phrase for "she flies with her own wings." Discovering this little gem written on my Albertson's shopping bag as I unloaded it from our van. My eyes finally catching the full scope of the brightly colored bag's design. Initially, the artist's vivid scenes of Portland, Oregon, distracted me from the writing encircling the base. As a native Oregonian of over 60 years, I may have already heard these Latin words before when studying the history of Oregon. On May 2, 1843, the Oregon Country settlers voted to make Alis Volat Propriis our state motto when forming a provisional government independent of the U.S. and Great Britain. Whether I learned this once before or not, these words are fresh and relevant— for my here and now.

May 1st will be indelibly etched in my mind as the day I lost my mother. Sorrowful thoughts of what life would be like without her deemed unbearable to ponder while she was alive; now they've become my altered and difficult reality. God's Word is a comfort to me and to all those who mourn, promising in

Psalm 27:13 MSG says, "I'm sure now I'll see God's goodness in the exuberant earth. Stay with God! Take heart. Don't quit. I'll say it again: Stay with God." His goodness descends from Heaven—gentle reminders of His love, lessening the chasm of grief and bringing comfort to my heart.

The day after my mama's passing, I wanted to get my mind off all that had happened, exhausted from Mom's illnesses, her death, and painful false accusations against me. I decided to watch an episode of American Idol that was recorded on May 1st. When the opening group song started, I could not believe my ears...they were singing a song about a mom telling her child to spread their butterfly wings and fly and not to waste their life worrying about what people say.

Tears streamed down my face, realizing God had sent me a message about my mama, encouraging me not follow in her footsteps of worrying about what people think of me. Now in Heaven, she is fully experiencing freedom from the fear of man that had become a snare; in Heaven's glory, she's liberated from earth's restrictions.

My journey toward audacious liberty began that very moment, albeit I didn't know it at the time. This butterfly message fluttered once again and came into view a couple of months later while my feet dangled out of the small opening into our attic. Staying seated close to the light, I sorted through the few boxes of my mom's belongings. Grieving her loss was more stifling than the attic's dense, windowless air.

While sifting through her stuff, I became saddened she had thrown out a lot of her belongings before she moved from her spacious apartment into one much smaller. One of those precious items I missed was her beloved roller skates, having fond memories of my brother Troy and I taking turns skating around in our basement as children. The list of missing items was long, realizing her dementia probably was a factor in her out-of-character decision to toss them.

Far beyond the scope of these earthly mementos was the loss of my parents. My soul felt darker than an orphan in the farthest corners of the attic. Intermittently, I wiped tears from my flushed face as I divided mementos into designated boxes for family members. As I continued to gently look through her belongings, I was suddenly surprised to see a bright pink butterfly on a 3x5 index card. Excitingly, I pulled it out to examine it closer. When I flipped the card over, it read: "All That the Father Hath Is Yours." And my dad added: "My Little Butterfly, —Love Al." My dad had written this to my mother on April 9th, 1977—one of the few things she kept that he'd given her. This orphan girl found solace in his simple yet powerful words

A few weeks after that profound discovery, my sweet BFF and her hubby surprised me and my husband as I celebrated my first birthday without my mama. Debbie crowned me with a birthday tiara and my eyes were masked to veil the secret of our destination. Once we arrived and mask was removed, I was handed tickets to the American Idol concert. Joy and excitement bubbled within me as we made our way into the coliseum to our amazing seats. We sat just in time to hear the familiar opening song, encouraging this butterfly to spread my wings and not waste my life.

God is over the top with His love and attention to detail, and Mama, you would be proud of me, for I'm learning the true meaning of Alis Volat Propriis.

Therefore we do not lose heart. Though outwardly we are wasting away, yet inwardly we are being renewed day by day. For our light and momentary troubles are achieving for us an eternal glory that far outweighs them all. —2 Corinthians 4:16–17 NIV

"Just when the caterpillar thought the world was over, it became a butterfly." —Chuang Tzu

"One can never consent to creep when one feels an impulse to soar." —Helen Keller

Prayer:
Lord, we thank you for the freedom You bring to our lives. When we are weighed down by a loss, rejection, fear, or shame, You are there.

Whatever the need, You long to set us free! Your Word promises us that those who You have set free are free, indeed. We praise You that we can fly with our own wings, because You not only created them, You are the wind beneath them.

An Absolute Peach

When I was a stay-at-home mom, my mother loved taking our young boys and I on grand adventures. Piling into her small white Nissan Sentra with a bag of munchies, we'd secure their car seats thoroughly and be ready to roll out onto the highway. Whether it was the beach the Dalles, Longview, or local malls, she loved to drive, and we loved to go. Exploring beyond the four walls of our small apartment was always a welcome treat.

When a long day of adventure was done, we'd pull into the driveway with sleepy boys, full tummies, and minds chock full of memories. Grandma's car interior usually revealed the aftermath of runaway graham crackers and toys from our magical getaways. Like clockwork, before you could say road trip, Grammy's car was cleaned out and ready for another exciting adventure.

My heart was overflowing with countless, funny, and precious memories from those splendid day trips. Packing two ladies with Lucille Ball tendencies into a compact car with young children was sure to produce some comedy gold! Now, as I gaze in the rearview mirror of the past, time seemed to have hit the acceleration pedal fast forward. Those once small boys now stand before us as grown men with facial hair, deep voices, and maturity that floods my heart with unspeakable love and gratitude. And knowing my mom is cheering from heaven...her most glorious trip ever is a comfort.

From time to time, those memories flutter into my mind, settling in on the stillness of our empty nest, bringing a smile to my face. It's a gift of extravagant love in our sometimes messy, broken, fumbling places. Love that shouts louder than failures, past or present, allows room for deeper, richer wholeness for me and my family. This love helps us learn to navigate on the expressway of grace and forgiveness.

I recently recalled one of those delightful memories of our impromptu trip to the Lloyd Center Mall one afternoon when they were small. The boys sat peacefully on the trip, paying little mind to the scenery, perfectly content with this short excursion. All was quiet on the home front until we rounded the bend, exposing very familiar surroundings. Our youngest son Trent declared from his car seat, with great delight, "Grandma, you're a peach, an absolute peach!" This winsome phrase came from a recently watched *Mr. Magoo* cartoon. My mom was beyond tickled, hoping to always be able to recall this adorable accolade.

My mom was not alone in her aptitude for adventure. The same God who spoke the world into existence, who tenderly formed you in your mother's womb, has the grandest adventure waiting for you just around the corner. We get the joy and privilege to partner with Him, calling dibs to ride shot gun with Jesus and the Holy Spirit for the ultimate ride of our lives.

God, Himself, is right alongside us, steady and on track with this spiritual adventure. I don't know what road you're traveling today. You could be cruising down the highway of life, tunes cranked and feeling carefree, or perhaps your road is lined with deep potholes of disappointment and despair. Maybe you're looking for a sign of hope to detour you from your present daunting circumstances.

Today, may you encounter God in a new fresh way, making your rough road smooth and the monotonous scenery explode with life and new-found possibilities.

And remember, "Though the path is difficult and the scenery dull at the moment, there are sparkling surprises just around the bend. Stay on the path I have selected for you. It is truly the path of life" (Sarah Young, *Jesus Calling*).

Stay the course God has mapped out for you, and in due season, I'm confident you will be declaring to God with great joy, "You're a peach— an absolute peach!"

The revelation of God is whole and pulls our lives together. The signposts of God are clear and point out the right road. The life-maps of God are right, showing the way to joy. The directions of God are plain and easy on the eyes. —Psalm 19:7–8 MSG

"A grand adventure is about to begin." —Winnie the Pooh

Prayer:
Lord, thank you that You are the God of turning rough roads smooth, restoring dashed hopes and dreams with more joy we could ever imagine. Doing life with You is the best road trip ever.

When You've Lost Your Passion

When we started our great room addition over 20 years ago, I was more than eager to gain some needed space to our 740-square-foot home. Finally, a dream kitchen that could accommodate two at once...what a concept! It would be nice to have a dishwasher that was not named *me*. Plus, ample counter space to actually allow us to leave the microwave out without removing it after each use would be wonderful. Those arduous microwave-lifting workouts to nuke a meal had me fearing my arm muscles would bulge to rival Popeye the sailor man's. Though that might be my husband's desired look for his biceps...not so much for me.

Though the pros to the addition were off the charts in comparison to any cons that loomed on the horizon, a few hiccups needed to be addressed. First of all, I had to gear myself up to the fact a good portion of the backyard landscape would be either dug up or covered in piles of dirt. Not only would it require me turning a blind eye to such mayhem, I would also need to relocate any plants I wished to save. Of all the chosen plants I hoped would survive was our Blue Passion flower. This glorious flower derived its name from the plant's ten petals and sepals representing the ten remaining faithful apostles. The flower's radial filaments suggest Jesus' crown of thorns and the three stigmas the nails that secured Him as He hung on the cross for humanity. What a beautiful reminder every time I stepped out my back door—its tangible canopy of love ushering me into my backyard and into glory.

To dig up and try to relocate this robust vine had me concerned I would lose this blooming memorial of God's grace. When the day came to transplant this large trailing plant, I whispered a hardy prayer that this vine would live. I believe in a God who cares about the big and the small things for His beloved children, even things we feel seem too trite. If it matters to you, it matters to God. So, I asked the God of the universe to have it not only survive the temporary bucket of foreign soil—while the foliage draped like a curtain over the swing set for support—but that it would flourish wherever I chose to relocate it.

Each day, as I peered out the kitchen window, reality harshly peered back; the vine's lush, green leaves turned brown and curled in protest to the new location. As the days rolled on with no sign of the plant rallying back, my denial that the plant could simply be in shock was no longer a viable option. Feeling a smidge of what Jonah must have felt when his broad-leafed vine that had brought him comfort and shade suddenly withered away, I, too, questioned God on this outcome. My heart was saddened the vine was unable to recover from this journey.

After several months of remodeling, there came a day when the dust settled, hammers stopped pounding, and the addition was complete. The new dishwasher hummed, and so did I; the stress of upheaval melted into celebration and a huge sigh of relief. However, unbeknownst to me as I was questioning and grieving the loss of my vine, God had already blown a seed of the passion from our previous vine over our roof to nestle securely by our side entry door. That seed grew with quantum leaps and bounds, far surpassing the previous vine, providing a canopy of splendor to all who entered. I marveled at the faithfulness of God when hope seems lost and prayers appear unanswered. That magnificent vine became a testimony that faith can indeed become sight and dormancy does not mean denial.

In order to get to God's true passion for our lives, things in the natural may need to shift or an unhealthy passion to die and be replaced and renewed in the proper soil of our hearts. Even though some strong passions may get buried in my life from time to time, God is in the business of resurrecting; He's calling forth new life that will be vital, thriving, and producing fruit from the Spirit and not my flesh.

His intentional, loving guidance is for the sole purpose of us living in a fuller more intimate walk with the lover of our souls.

Psalm 92:13-15 AMPC promises us that we will be "...planted in the house of the Lord, they shall flourish in the courts of our God. (Growing in grace) they shall still bring forth fruit in old age; they shall be full of sap (of spiritual vitality) and (rich in the verdure (of trust, love, and contentment)."

"A state of mind that sees God in everything is evidence of growth in grace and a thankful heart." —Charles Finney

Prayer:

Heavenly Father, thank you for Your tender loving care. You always bring new life and new passion for living, even when we experience loss and don't see any immediate beauty with what is happening in our present circumstances. Thank you, Jesus, that Your passion for us never dies even when we don't see or feel it.

Entwined Hearts

Recently, it dawned on me that jokingly calling the word "wait" a four-letter word was not a good idea. There have been times in my life when waiting felt like a long prison sentence with no hope of parole and no visitor called Joy. This mindset's root cause was my lack of trust and complete confidence in God's faithfulness. Not only that, my thoughts were skipping the biblical principles of Philippians 4:9 AMPC: "Rejoice in the Lord always [delight, gladden yourselves in Him]; again I say, Rejoice!" It encourages us to rejoice and trust. My false notion in regards to waiting was conceived, birthed, and nursed on lies.

This narrative continued to grow out of a lack of trust in God's goodness. Doubt became the framework of my wobbly emotional structure, which proved insufficient building materials to fully lean on God's goodness in my times of waiting. Removing the core nature of God's faithfulness from the equation of waiting, I was choosing to be dictated by feelings over faith, which will fail any faith-building inspection.

I'm reminded of Peter's bold steps to walk on water as Jesus bid him, only to suddenly let his fear and doubt stop him in his water tracks and sink him. I love what Matthew 14:31 NIV says: "Immediately Jesus reached out his hand and caught him. 'You of little faith,' he said, 'why did you doubt?'"

So, why did Peter's bold step of faith to meet Jesus abruptly stop? He saw the wind and crashing waves against the boat he just stepped out of, where the other 11 apostles were waiting. Peter's fear of the wind caused him to take His eyes off Jesus, gripping his heart with doubt causing him to sink—even though Jesus had comforted His fearful disciples only moments before in verse 27 while He was walking on the water, saying, "Take courage! It is I. Don't be afraid." I'm comforted to know that even Peter doubted in the waiting, letting sight override faith, allowing doubt to drown him. All this despite Jesus living among them on a daily basis with unwavering faithfulness. Like me, the whirlwind of circumstances deceived him, while the wind of adversity whipped up fear that raged in his soul.

Also, I find it interesting that in Matthew Chapter 14, three different occasions when Jesus did something for his disciples, immediately afterward a juxtaposition took place. The value of waiting is seen. Check it out for a great read. God is a God of waiting and a God of suddenlies. Though I love the suddenlies, there is great significance in the waiting, allowing the necessary work of the Holy Spirit within our own hearts and minds to be done while we wait. James W. Goll writes, "When the fullness of preparation meets the fullness of time, it results in the culture or atmosphere where suddenlies come to pass."

The bottom line remains, "He has made everything beautiful in its time,"(Ecclesiastes 3:11 ESV). This reality of God's truth empowers us to take a position of rejoicing in His exceedingly great and precious promise even while we wait.

As I repented for my four-letter word definition of WAIT, the Lord brought to mind the countless scripture verses that celebrate waiting.

The truth is, we not only wait on Him, He waits on us.
To surrender our will for His.
To lay on the altar those things we cling to.

Offering our bodies as living sacrifices holy and pleasing to God. A beautiful exchange of earthly pleasures for His far greater Kingdom purposes.

It reminds me of a tall curly willow branch propped up behind our shed waiting to be used, while in its stillness a glorious honeysuckle nearby seeking additional support, twirled around the dead lifeless branch.

Gracefully, beautifully entwining its purpose with life and destiny.

Yet the LORD longs to be gracious to you; therefore he will rise up to show you compassion. For the LORD is a God of justice. Blessed are all who wait for him! —Isaiah 30:18 NIV

Perhaps you, too, are tired of being on the team where wait is a four-letter word. Are you ready for a shift into freedom? I know I am!

"...me, I'm not giving up. I'm sticking around to see what God will do. I'm waiting for God to make things right. I'm counting on God to listen to me. Spread your wings!" —Micah 7:7 MSG

"Our willingness to wait reveals the value we place on the object we're waiting for." —Charles Stanley

Prayer:
Jesus, today I feel like a dead branch waiting for a promise or a purpose. Help me, Lord, to see Your goodness in the waiting. May I entwine myself in Your love and ever-faithful promises. I know I will be forever changed in the process, as beauty will burst forth from the waiting.

God's Grace for Every Season

 **Summer**

He is like a tree planted by water, that sends out its roots by the stream, and does not fear when heat comes, for its leaves remain green, and is not anxious in the year of drought, for it does not cease to bear fruit. —Jeremiah 17:8 MSG

Pocket full of Promises

What has the Lord been showing you in this summer season?

_____

_____

_____

_____

_____

Write a one-word take away to describe this season.

_____

It was you who set all the boundaries of the earth; you made both summer and winter. —Jeremiah 74:17 NIV

"I believe in Christianity as I believe that the sun has risen: not only because I see it, but because by it I see everything else."
—C.S. Lewis

He is like a tree planted by streams of water that yields its fruit in its season, and its leaf does not wither. In all that he does, he prospers.
—Psalm 1:3 ESV

"Autumn is a second spring when every leaf is a flower."
—Albert Comus

Closer to God

Whenever my mom would share something exciting that the Lord had done for her, she would more than likely end her story with, "I'm so excited I could jump up and click my heels!" Then, quickly followed it with, "But I'm afraid I might fall and break my hip." Afterward, she would give a chuckle, and I would smile at all her amusement.

She'd also share about how she longed to go up to the Columbia River Gorge and praise the Lord over the breathtaking scenery. Most of the time, my mom talked of this while visiting our home; afterward, she would walk out onto our small deck along the north side of our home. As her feet landed on the wood planks, she would lift her arms, thanking and praising God. Returning inside, quite content, her face beamed, and she would gush about how much she enjoyed the deck that Kevin built. Our modest deck with no sweeping views seemed to satisfy my mom's yearning to stand outside and give God glory. Whether or not I accompanied her as she extoled our adoring Creator, in the back of my mind, I longed to someday take my mother to her "dream spot."

Years went by with only my good intentions. She never got to stand and worship the lover of her soul at The Gorge...until one day. The sun was shining, the air crisp, and leaves were ablaze. Vivid hues formed a pleasant parade route up the scenic highway, welcoming her long-awaited arrival. Arm in arm, Kevin and I escorted her to drink in the panoramic view and to finally stand in the place she'd always dreamed about. Praise rolled off her tongue as she looked at all the beauty our Heavenly Father created. While standing next to her, I was hungry to hear every word that Mom uttered. Though it was hard to leave her side, I managed to pull myself away to get a couple of photos to remember this day. It wasn't long before the sun slowly began to subside, and the chill of the air nudged us to bring this remarkable event to a close. Thus, it was time to gingerly help my mom back into the warm cozy car for our trip home.

Leaves danced and twirled in celebration as we wound our way back down the old scenic highway, holding warm memories of our splendid day together in our hearts. It was a prolonged dream realized.

We beheld the work of a God who makes all things beautiful in His time—a brilliant and glorious crescendo with the best seats in the house. In humbleness, we offered our God a well-deserved standing ovation poised on holy ground. Filled with deep appreciation and gratitude, we watched my mother's desire fulfilled: to stand closer to God.

The heavens declare the glory of God; the skies proclaim the work of his hands. —Psalm 19:1 NIV

"I love to think of nature as an unlimited broadcasting station, through

which God speaks to us every hour, if we will only tune in."
—George Washington Carver

Prayer:
Lord, thank you for making all things beautiful in Your time. You are never late or too early for Your plans to unfold. When we feel like we miss the mark, remind us that with You, we are right on target.

Met in a Mosh Pit

During one particular day while praying for our two sons to know God's love more completely, my soul was stirred to read Psalm 19:1 AMPC. The first few verses captured me as I read, "The heavens declare the glory of God; the firmaments shows and proclaims His handiwork. Day after day pours forth speech and night after night shows forth knowledge."

Quickly, my thoughts envisioned how they would see God's love. Maybe the countless celestial stars would blink, declaring "I love you!" Or could a glowing, majestic moon reveal this captivating message? Perhaps the infinite marvels of nature would point straight to their loving Creator.

Several days after that devotion, it was time to take our youngest son and some friends to the "Demon Hunter" concert...complete with a mosh pit! That night, my prayer included an extra protection clause for safety. Somehow, the words "mosh pit" conjure up all sorts of unpleasant images—one of the downsides of thinking creatively.

Thankfully, after the concert was over, all the boys piled back into our van safe, sound, and full of stories to tell. Our son Trent recounted the evening, sharing about the confined crowds and a particular young man dancing with reckless abandonment across the room from him. Shortly after Trent noticed him, he realized that the sweaty, carefree dancer was standing right alongside him. Trent decided to ask if he was okay, to which he replied, "Yeah, man, I'm just praying for you." This man spoke into our son's life with insight and clarity, speaking hope and encouragement, doing so with pinpoint accuracy. He then closed with, "Just a little FYI for you from the Creator of the universe," and quickly returned back to his original location, all the while moshing with tremendous flair.

After Trent finished his story, my eyes welled up with tears, remembering my prayer for our children to see God's love as a Creator. Thoughts of crashing waves, warm sunshine, or snow-covered mountain peaks came to mind. Then, I was reminded that God pours forth His speech and knowledge without limitations or impediments, full of compassion and creativity—more than willing to meet us in a loud, stuffy, and overcrowded mosh pit. Unknowingly, my thoughts and ways painted a thumbnail picture when I needed a canvas to capture the image of a God with no restrictions. Portraying His true nature, the Creator of the cosmos stands by us no matter where we find ourselves. His rapturous ways and thoughts are higher than heaven, earth, and our own.

Today, may you feel His adoring love. Whether you are on one of life's impressive pinnacles or in the impoverished pits, God is with you! And to coin the passionate mosher's phrase, "Just a little FYI from the Creator of the universe."

"A God wise enough to create me and the world I live in is wise enough to watch out for me." —Philip Yancey

Prayer:
God, we praise You for Your glorious creation. Thank you for declaring Your love to us in creative and delightful ways. May we never miss a detail of Your kindness, love, or mercy for our behalf.

Konnichiwa to Peace

Our son Derek and his friend were going on trip of a lifetime: a two-week vacation in Tokyo. In Tokyo, they'd be beholding all the sights and sounds of a rich culture, not to mention it being an electronic mecca. If anyone knows me in the ever so slightest way, they would know this trip was not going to be a cake walk for me. In all the years of being a mother, I had battled intense fears, foreboding thoughts of possible abuse, kidnappings, accidents, or sicknesses and all the alarming stuff in the middle. In fact, if you can name it, I probably have feared it. Been there, done that.

I would imagine any loving mother has combated some of the same fears for her children. It's a natural desire to nurture and protect our babies, no matter how old they are. However, for me it went far beyond normal trepidation a caring parent would have; at times it became irrational and larger-than-life, going so far as to cripple me from releasing our sons to go anywhere with anyone—even their own father—for years. Words cannot begin to express how incredibly hard this was for my husband, children, and me. I simply felt helpless to break free.

Looking back, after having come to greater depths of healing in this area, I marvel and am utterly humbled that Kevin stayed married to me. Through those layers of painful growth came revelation to why my fears where at critical mass; some were fostered from past personal sexual abuse I was aware and unaware of. Buried deep, pushed down by stratum of shame, denial and trauma manifested itself through unhealthy behaviors.

Today, I'm so thankful to God who has shown me His perfect love that casts out fear and for my husband and children who endured the strain of my intense struggles for freedom with their love and forgiveness. Plus, where would I be without the love and support of mentors and friends who've also walked with me through it all. And though they did not wrestle the same degree of debilitating demons as I, they chose to stand by me in my brokenness. Loving me without judgment, they offered me compassion and grace that became a breeding ground for my healing. Whenever I mustered up strength to take a baby step, they applauded with such exuberance you'd think I had run a marathon and was the first to break the finishing-line ribbon.

My sons are grown adults now, and do I still worry about them? I sure do! But nowhere near the unhealthy, crippling fear I once battled. For I have learned the freedom of trusting God more fully.

Today, whether your taking quantum leaps of faith or faltering baby steps, God applauses them both, He delights in each step or leap you take toward Him. Cheering you on, it does not matter where your starting line begins. He rejoices with you at your victorious finish.

You will guard him and keep him in perfect and constant peace whose mind [both its inclination and its character] is stayed on You, because he commits himself to You, leans on You, and hopes confidently in You. —Isaiah 26:3 AMPC

"He is our peace; he came to bring it, and he left it behind him as he went away." —Charles Spurgeon

Prayer:
Father, we praise You, in awe of Your delight for us and the comfort You bring in our storm-tossed seas, providing perfect peace as our mind stays on You, trusting You over the mounding waves of fear. Learning to say sayonara (goodbye) to fear, we can say kon'nichiwa (hello) to peace.

The Journey of a Thousand Little Goodbyes

Saying goodbye to those we love is never easy. It will undoubtedly tug strongly on our heart strings, and if it's final, well, that will be far beyond a yank. Goodbyes can pull our heart to its breaking point due to the forcible impact of our loss. As time marches on and my years head towards the golden, I'm painfully aware that saying goodbye will be woven more frequently and tightly as the lives around me come to an end or relationships, sadly, dissolve.

One day, I listened to Amy Grant's song called "Better Not to Know."

As she sang about seasons coming and going, goodbyes more than hellos, she ponders perhaps it's better not to know the timing.

I've asked myself that question when life has dealt me blindsiding blows and sent me reeling, my mind spinning into a flurry of *whys?* Oh, I know I'm not supposed to ask the *why* question, but I do. I compare pictures I had in my mind of my future to the one I have been given. Strangely, they rarely look the same. I search for God in the sea of chaos like a "Where's Waldo" image, straining to see Him in my overcrowded crestfallen circumstances. Instead of looking for Waldo's striped shirt and beanie, I look for God—His nail-scarred hands and feet, wounds He bore for you and me.

Isaiah 53:5 AMPC says, "But He was wounded for our transgressions, He was bruised for our guilt and iniquities; the chastisement (needful to obtain) peace and well-being for us was upon Him, and with the stripes (that wounded) Him we are healed and made whole."

And then my eyes see Him. He was there all along, never failing or forsaking me. Sometimes it feels like He is hidden in plain view, surrounded by life's beautiful messes, joy, sadness, and triumphs mingled with tragedy. And even when my mind floods with questions and doubt, God prevails. We don't have to live long to know that death can come suddenly, with no warning, no chance for farewells, or proper send off. Or it may come in what I call "The Journey of a Thousand Little Goodbyes." These exist in the slow, day-to-day departures from what was once normal, watching loved ones slip away, one painful closure at a time. We greet the dawning of a new day not knowing what part of their personality and capabilities will be gone forever. And while you hold onto every essence of who they are in that moment, in a blink of an eye it shifts yet again, finding yourself saying goodbye once more.

We say so long to what was normal and familiar, sinking into grief, weighty sorrow, and sadness that can pull you down into a tomorrow that seems bleaker than today. Irretrievable grains of "used to be's" envelope us.

An excruciating truth confronts us, that...
One day, your loved one can no longer call you or give you a hug.
One day, they can no longer brush their teeth, comb their hair, dress, or feed themselves.
One day, they can no longer walk, tell you they love you, or fill the air with laughter.
And then, one day, they are gone... forever in this life time.

In losing my family members so far, it has been a "Journey of Thousand Little Goodbyes." First, it was losing my dad at the age of 27 to cancer, six months after his diagnosis. Fast forward 25 years later, my thousand farewells began again with my mama as her dementia and congestive heart failure chipped away at her strong body and vibrant personality. While at the same time, my only sibling was fighting his personal battle with Lewy Body dementia dove tailed Mom's illness. Waves of loss washed over me as my mother and brother needed help to get into the car, buckle their seat belts, form words, or be their memory. I silently mourned a family I would never see whole again until we all reunite in Heaven.

My journey of thousand little goodbyes became final goodbyes for both my mom and brother here on earth, and though I did not know what the future held, I knew who held my future.

The Lord gave this verse as my brother's final days came to a close.

The right-living people are out of their misery, they're finally at rest.
They lived well and with dignity, and now they're finally at peace.
—Isaiah 57:2 MSG

My heart selfishly wanted them here with me, and yet they had fought the good fight and were ready to be with Jesus. This verse was spot on and such a comfort to me.

I don't know what goodbyes you've had to face—if they were sudden or drawn out—but I do know God wants to bring you comfort in every grief-stricken situation—past, present, or future..

He heals the brokenhearted and binds up their wounds.
—Psalm 147:3 NIV

"Yesterday is history, tomorrow is a mystery, today is a gift, that is why we call it the present." —Bill Keane

Prayer:
God, thank you that You hold on tightly to our hands, saying, "Fear not, I will help you." Your love and faithfulness are a shield round about us. When we walk through the fire, we will not be burned, and through the floods we will not drown. Your grace covers us "when it's better not to know."

Grace-Filled Storms

The sun was shining brilliantly outside my window while powerful winds relentlessly tossed trees seemingly without mercy. Inside, my feet dangled freely and rather comfortably positioned right over a toasty heat register, unaware of the robust gales outside. As I pondered these mighty winds our beloved city of Troutdale is known for displaying, I've concluded that Chicago could have strong competition holding the title of "The Windy City" if it was ever up for grabs. This little town is proving to be one heck of a powerful contender thanks to the east winds whipping through the Columbia River Gorge. If, by chance, we were in Christopher Robin's neck of the woods, Winnie the Pooh would call this a "blustery day" indeed. However, my mind was contemplating and pondering more than the breeze that rattled the windows; I wondered what the rest of the day was to hold. My spirits were being churned just like the unsettled blasts of winds a mere stone's throw from my cozy indoor haven.

Later that day, my husband and I had plans to visit my brother at his Alzheimer's care facility where he resides. Each visit I braced myself, expecting to experience storm-tossed, squally feelings of loss. Deep longing for days gone by hit me. I longed for when my brother and I could laugh and communicate more freely—far before illness graffitied words such as *limitation* on the walls of his life. Through it all, I tried to hear the heart of God over my redundant and deafening questions of *why*. Why this Lord? Why now? Why him? Aware for now these why questions are left unanswered.

Regardless, I knew I was not alone. Many of you can relate to the wrestling thoughts of your personal *whys*. Maybe it's the *why* of an illness, a painful divorce, a heartbreaking death, or some other tragic loss. Perhaps you don't ask the why's like I do, being aware that focusing on them is usually not helpful. There's a key to greater understanding: when I pause to fix my gaze at the bigger picture called eternity... glimmering with all its truth. One of my favorite songs at the time was Laura Story's song, "Blessings," telling the listener that maybe our disappointments, the storms that toss us about, are truly God mercies in disguise. Laura wrote "Blessings" after a brain tumor hospitalized her husband in 2006. It was a stormy time for them, and so was the road to recovery that followed. When being interviewed by Kevin Davis of

NRT, she shared, "The song shows that we still have more questions than answers. But there's a decision that I find God is asking us to make. Are we going to judge God based on our circumstances, or are we going to choose to interpret our circumstances based on what we hold to be true about God?"

Walking in a temporal world repeatedly asking the whys tosses my soul back and forth, blasting my faith with its billowing windstorms. Speaking from experience, I have a battered soul to prove it. However, today, I can choose to walk again with a determined faith making a sincere conscious effort to take each day as a gift. Because God's mercies are new every morning, I'm embracing more completely the here and now with all the messes and heartache that can accompany it, trying my best to refrain from asking a copious amount of the journalist questions to God—the Who, What, When, Where, Why, How's. Instead, I'm asking this: "What is it that You are trying to teaching me, Lord?"

If we know who God is and His promises, the When, Where, Why, and How will lose prominence. God is love, God is just, God is faithful, to name a few. We can boldly look to Jesus, the Author and Finisher of our faith. Whether it's sunny, windy, or both, we can rejoice, turning our maze of questions into an amazing trust, painting grace graffiti on the fences of our limitations and losses.

I call to you, God, because I'm sure of an answer. So-answer!
Bend your ear! listen sharp! Paint grace graffiti on the fences...
—Psalm 17:6-7 MSG

"For the Present is the point at which time touches eternity."
—C.S. Lewis

Prayer:
Lord, thank you; You know how much I need You. Your truth, grace, and joy are my only hope in the storm-tossed sea of *whys*. May I choose to cast all my cares upon You, for I know You care for me.

Flying the Friendly Skies

September 2015 was the month of firsts—the first time I had stepped on a plane in 29 long years, the first time my husband had ever flown (with the exception of a puddle jumper as a child), and now our family's first trip to Disney World. Fear had a way of paralyzing me through the years, making me partly or wholly incapable of movement in certain areas of my life. My fear-riddled thoughts pooled up in a depraved ecosystem of *what if's*, incapable to produce true liberty or a full, abundant life like Christ promises.

Yet, the older I get, the more I want all God has for me. It's time to fear less and fly more, allowing my spirit to soar. Though this is a mere dress rehearsal for all of glorious eternity, I still want to learn to push fear aside to enjoy the ride along the way. Hunter S. Thompson wrote, "Life should not be a journey to the grave with intentions of arriving safety in a pretty and well-preserved body, but rather to skid in broadside in a cloud of smoke, thoroughly used up totally worn out and loudly proclaiming Wow! What a ride!"

No doubt I will not be doing any death-defying feats like jumping out of an airplane anytime soon; flying in a plane seems to suffice at the moment.

Before our vacation, the Lord gave me a song to tuck away in my heart weeks before the trip, like a Papa Daddy hug to His worried daughter. Fittingly, the song was from the Disney film *Aladdin*: "A Whole New World."

Aladdin sung this amazing song to Jasmine while soaring over sights and sounds on their magical carpet ride. If you ever listen to this song, I encourage you to think of the Lord singing it to you. It will absolutely touch your heart.

God does want to show us a new world, filled with wonder and new points of view, encouraging us to not close our eyes from seeing all that He has to give us.

Before we left, I listened to this song countless times. Whether it was Sandi Patty and David Phelps or Aladdin, to me it felt like the Lord was singing over me again and again.

And while high in the sky I whispered this song too while gazing out the window. It was such a powerful healing time for me. And while on the ground in Disney World's Epcot Center, God's kindness greeted us back from the air. His love letter was written in the sky, as a plane flew 10,000 feet skywriting "Jesus Loves You" for all of Disney World to see.

Flying the friendly skies with Jesus and His comforting words are a game changer. His Word promises in Psalm 121:2-8 NIV:

My help comes from the Lord, who made heaven and earth. He will not allow your foot to slip or to be moved; He Who keeps you will not slumber. Behold, He who keeps Israel will neither slumber nor sleep. The Lord is your keeper; the Lord is your shade on your right hand [the side not carrying a shield]. The sun shall not smite you by day, nor the moon by night. The Lord will keep you from all evil; He will keep your life. The Lord will keep your going out and your coming in from this time forth and forevermore.

Whether on land, sky, or sea, He is with you always. What whole new world does God want to show you?

Be glad, good people, fly to God! —Psalm 64:9-10 MSG

"Fear not tomorrow. God is already there." —Ruth Graham

Prayer:
Jesus, how you love us! We thank you for writing in the sky and in our

hearts. Your love letters speak to fear and loss with comfort and grace. We praise You for Your tender loving care toward all Your children.

What the Beep?

The beautiful, stately beach house stood perched on a hill with sweeping panoramic views; this lovely rental was our new location for our annual "Hugs" Bible study retreat. Bea, our fearless coordinator for the yearly trip, painstakingly peruses the internet for a home that can accommodate up to 11 ladies, has easy beach access, and comfy interior surroundings, all without costing us an arm and a leg. Along with her spearheading all the necessary incidentals and food, which rivals an all-you-can-eat buffet, it's a job that's not for the faint of heart!

At this particular home, Bea's concern was the limited parking and the steepness of the hill on which we needed to park. Due to the confined space, I offered to use my trusty seven-passenger van for a carpool. It had been years since I had volunteered, and though I'm not a big fan of driving to places less traveled, I thought this would be a jolly good time to do it. Conquering fear and trepidation with a van full of loving, gracious souls who will pray with a passion is a guaranteed recipe for overcoming life's challenges.

The ride there was delightful with lots of laughs. We had our traditional stop at Annette's for lunch, and before you knew it we were beginning to ascend the steep hill to our home away from home in Lincoln City on the beautiful Oregon Coast. Upon arrival, we realized the hill was indeed steep, the road narrow, and the website touting space to park three cars actually translated into one car that needed to be like a circus clown's. Overshadowing all these minor details was a glorious home beckoning us to open the door to savor the treasures inside. Giddy, we unloaded the cars, settled into our cozy rooms, and embraced the oceanfront views the steep hill brought us to.

That weekend was a rich time of sharing a temporary home with remarkable women who love God with such fervor and unwavering devotion. Unfolding before my eyes, was their tremendous love and care for their families and friends—a glorious enduring display of grace and unconditional love. With a steadfast commitment to weather life's storms, they were confident in a Savior who calms every tempest that crashes against their souls. It's such a relaxing and inspirational getaway that always ends far too quickly.

Such was the case as we bustled about on our final day, packing up our belongings and tidying up the rental, then gathering for our customary group photo. Closing our splendid time with a prayer and the traditional hootenanny (that is worthy of a story all on its own), we hugged and said our goodbyes. In all the revelries of the weekend, I seem to forget that I parked up the hill even further to allow friends who arrived later to park in the driveway. With that realization came some apprehension of backing out of such tight conditions.

After saying a quiet prayer to myself, my traveling buddies, Lynn and Susy, piled into the car. Backing up with an *I got this attitude*, I no sooner heard a loud and disturbing crunch. I had backed into a wood pile and bottomed out the car. With each new attempt I tried, I could not get past the obstacle. Seeing my need, Liz and Sharon approached the van—Liz fearlessly guided the front of my car while Sharon courageously navigated the back. All the while, my van's tires were losing traction and spinning and the ultra-sensitive backup warning beeped incessantly at this added intrusion. The rain poured down, drenching my friends, and my nerves unraveled at each unsuccessful jockeying for position. With the help of encouraging, prayerful copilots and Liz and Sharon's enduring patience and loving guidance, I was finally able to get enough traction to pull up and away from the impediment.

Isn't that a picture of God's love? Tireless, unwavering love that guides us through storms while taking the brunt to bring our freedom, cheering us on with passionate encouragement, awakening our souls to a hope that does not disappoint, just like His Word promises.

I am eternally grateful for God's redemption that has saved me from the depths of despair. His love radically changed me and continues to every time I chose to embrace Him.

This profound love gift is also wrapped up in our family and friends who come alongside to partner with us in life's ups and downs. When emotional wheels spin and obstacles prevent us from experiencing His peace and purposes for our lives, Christ through them becomes the traction to propel us to our destiny.

My heart exceedingly rejoices in His tremendous unfailing love—in the freedom found and the promise of more. The beautiful gifts of family and friends are heart strings of grace to the tune of God's melodious love—a harmonious antidote to the incessant clamor of those ever-intrusive beeps of life. Experiencing His peace and purposes for our lives, Christ through them becomes the traction to propel us to our destiny.

I thank my God every time I remember you. In all my prayers for all of you, I always pray with joy... —Philippians 1:3-4 NIV

"Things are never quite as scary when you've got a best friend"
—Bill Watterson

Prayer:
Lord, thank you for delightful, loving friends and family who help lighten our load. Whether it's a smile, hug, prayer, or encouragement, they are a gift from You.

Hold You Me

When Trent, our youngest son, was a toddler, I would gaze down at that precious cherub face, gently framed by his golden locks of hair, and ask him, "Do you want Mommy to hold you?" especially when he seemed in need of a snuggle of comfort or reassurance. With his nod of approval, he would be swooped up in my loving arms with sheer delight, both of us embracing the joy of the tender moment. More often than not, he was content and fully engaged in life with endless bounds of energy and no need for Mommy to hold him. He had places to go, people to see, and by golly things to do.

When I go through Trent's childhood photos, it is safe to say there are way more photos of him it motion than sitting still. Yet, every now and then, his little spirit needed comfort, and if I was busy and not as keen to his needs, he would come to my side and tug on my clothing or wrap his arms around my leg. He'd look up with his brown eyes and squeezable cheeks saying, "Mommy, hold you me." My heart would melt at his adorable rendition of my all-to-familiar question, and soon he would be in my arms greeted with a kiss and the comfort he longed for. "Mommy, hold you me" is one of my all-time favorite sayings during his toddler years, and one I draw on as a spiritual lesson as well.

Hold you me is like saying what Matthew 22:39 NIV tells us: "...love your neighbor as yourself."

One colossal hurdle for me has been the journey of learning to love myself. Crippling low self-esteem and a distorted body image led me on a painful journey. Through the years, I have been ruthless—unyielding to extend grace or unconditional love to myself. Instead, I allowed a grueling taskmaster to hammer at my soul without mercy, punishing every flaw and imperfection, begging it to submit to the unattainable idol of perfection. Though I could love and forgive others in my limited capacity, I could never seem to extend that luxury to myself.

Looking back now, I allowed so many people to speak negativity into my life, which is so sad. I'm still learning to love me as I snuggle up in the arms of a profoundly loving God, tuning my heart to hear His heart and thoughts toward me, His beloved daughter. Just as Trent needed that reassuring comfort and love from me.

When a scribe asked Jesus which commandment is the first and principal of all, Jesus answered, "The first is to love the Lord your God with all your heart, soul, mind and strength. The second is to love your neighbor as yourself. There is no other commandment greater than these" (Mark 12:30-31 AMP, my paraphrase).

"The scribe admired and embraced the truth Jesus laid out, and when Jesus saw that he answered intelligently (discreetly and having his wits about him) He said, 'You are not far from the Kingdom of God.' Loving God out of and with our whole heart and out of and with all our soul (your life) and out of and with all your mind (your faculty of thought and your moral understanding) and out of and with all your strength" (Mark 12:32-33 AMP, my paraphrase).

Oh to not be far from the Kingdom of God—such freedom! He wants all of our heart, soul, mind, and strength. When we press into Him, we are comforted and loved with the deepest love that goes to the core of our being, bringing healing and wholeness into every nook and cranny of brokenness. How can love for ourselves and others not flow out from that rich abundance?

Such profound revelations from the mouth of a babe. Now, with that resounding love and freedom, I have places to go, people to love, and by golly things to do! Please join me as we have Jesus "Hold You Me."

Even if my father and mother abandon me, the Lord will hold me close. —Psalm 27:10 NLT

"Give away a breathtaking amount of grace. We have an endless supply since it comes from an infinite source. Live in grace, walk in love." —Bob Goff

Prayer:

Lord, we thank you for Your abounding love and for Your Word that tells us "How precious and weighty also are Your thoughts to me, O God! How vast is the sum of them! If I could count them, they would be more in number than the sand. When I awoke, (could I count to the end) I would still be with You" (Psalm 139:17–18 AMPC). Amen and amen.

Worth More than Rose Gold

One thing you should know about me is that I'm in love with rose gold. This slight infatuation increased one hundredfold on our trip to Disneyland in 2019. While there, I was met with a sea of sparkly rose gold Minnie Mouse ears. My heart skipped a beat for these glittering beauties, but I had already made a hard and fast rule long before we planted our feet in the Magic Kingdom. My foolproof plan was to purchase my Minnie Mouse ears online before our vacation ever started. Obviously by doing so I would save money and reduce the temptation to overspend while there. While I highly recommend this strategy, the best laid plans can still go south.

When the bargain ears arrived, they were either way too small or way too big. However, I remained fully committed to wearing them without bothering to check if they were returnable. Growing up, I often heard "waste not, want not," and perhaps it was this notion that convinced me that those bargain babies were getting packed up and going with us regardless of whether they looked ridiculous or not. Honestly, Disneyland is filled with ridiculous items you can place on your head anyway—one of the many things I love about the place.

When we finally arrived at the park, Kevin encouraged me to buy something for myself. Even though I loved most of what I saw, I was far from in love with the price tags. So, my admirable response was a polite, "No, thank you."

Until...

One lustrous day, those rose gold Minnie Mouse ears finally broke down my frugality with their magnetic, glittering glory. Like a thrifty moth to the uneconomical flame, I was drawn to the display. I picked one up, just to gaze at its charming allure, and my husband wasted no time in insisting I get them. The poor guy had been watching me wearing micro or macro Minnie ears each day as we strolled in the park, and he was more than ready to bless me. Just when I was about to take the purchase plunge, I turned in the cashier's direction and froze.

Tears suddenly welled up. Delicate, graceful tears for the record. No ugly crying (this time).

Seeing my tears, Kevin tenderly asked, "What's wrong?" I looked at him and simply said, "I don't deserve them."

In the forefront of my mind were all my failures and the fears I had been battling during our trip. These had left me grumpy in the middle of the Happiest Place on Earth. And the truth is, I didn't deserve them.

Despite the truth of my confession, Kevin lovingly took the ears from my hand and marched up to the counter like a man on a mission. I stood there speechless and in awe as the guilt melted away. When he returned, he placed in my hands the most gorgeous set of Minnie Mouse ears this girl has ever laid eyes on. It was a beautiful act of grace. Although I had been acting in ugly ways and deserving a far different outcome, he chose to forgive me and clothe me in beauty.

The truth is, none of us deserve anything good. We certainly don't deserve what God has so willingly and freely given us. "But God shows his love for us in that while we were still sinners, Christ died for us" Romans 5:8 ESV.

While we were still sinners...Christ died for us.

We are all sinners saved only by God's redeeming grace. God's love through the cross proved His unmerited mercy and favor toward us. We can choose to accept His free gift of salvation and forgiveness and to walk in humility, repentance, and thanksgiving. Once we acknowledge our failure and choose to trust in Him, He clothes us with new identity and worth.

My husband's grace and generosity spoke the love of God in a language I could understand. God knows how to speak directly to your heart. Ask Him to show you His love. You may feel God's love when you see a beautiful sunset, when you get a helping hand, or when you hear encouraging words. For many, getting a trinket like Minnie ears would not have touched your heart the way it did mine! The beautiful thing is, God knows our unique love languages, and we learn His love language when read His Word—a love letter to us. As you read it, I highly encourage you to journal His powerful truths and loving thoughts toward you. Let them sink deep into your spirit.

See what kind of love the Father has given to us, that we should be called children of God; and so we are. —1 John 3:1 ESV

"Adults are only kids grown up anyway." —Walt Disney

Prayer:
Heavenly Father, Your love is a powerful, unwavering force that grabs our hearts and won't let us go. Thank you that we are so deeply loved, not for what we do but how we are in You.

You've Got Mail

When our boys were five and seven years old, one of my prayers for them was to have a dog. Growing up, my brother and I had a lot of fond

131

memories of Herbie, our little poodle mix. As parents, my husband and I wanted our children to have some special moments similar to ours growing up. Although we wrestled with the fact our money was tight and our cottage home small—a tight situation on both ends—I began praying, asking God for a dog with these specifications: a little dog that was also CHEAP. I was trusting in a God who loves to give us the desires of our heart.

One day while answering the phone, I was delighted to hear my bubbly friend and mentor Michelle's voice. In her trademark cheerful tone mixed with passionate zeal, she exclaimed, "Guess what, Lisa!?" To which I replied, "What?!" trying to reach her level of enthusiasm. She chimed in with such exuberance it could have motivated a failing football team into the state championships.

"God says 'You've got mail," she said eagerly, making me laugh at her perky statement. Being a routinely self-confessing Eeyore from time to time, I greatly appreciated having a Tigger bouncing around to lift my occasional drooping spirits.

After our conversation ended, there was a newfound spring in my step faintly resembling that of "T I DOUBLE GER" throughout my day's errands. Finishing up that afternoon with a trip to our neighborhood post office, I amused myself while waiting in line by reading the signs below the counter. An unfamiliar sign was posted that caught my eye which simply read: "Lost dog, ask clerk." When it came time to step up to the counter, my casual statement to the clerk was, "Oh, how's the lost dog doing?" trying to engage her in a brief exchange of pleasantries, She didn't miss a beat by replying, "Would you like us to bring her over to your house today?" I'm like whoa! That was not what I was expecting to hear, neither was I expecting to hear myself blurt out an unwavering, "Yes." Walking away from the counter, I wondered what just happened.

That same day at 3:00 p.m., a sweet mail carrier brought over a puppy cute as a button. It was a Blue Heeler/Border Collie with a splash of

Corgi in the mix, all dressed up in a striking black and white coat. Upon opening the front door, this little cutie wasted no time cleaning up a bounty of cheerios the boys had spilled on the living room floor. This act alone sealed the deal for me. Her efficient clean up worked better than any vacuum cleaner I ever owned, making Kirby, Hoover, or Dyson completely fitting names if my husband agreed to keep this lovable pooch. A petite four-legged creature, she became fast friends with the boys and I, waiting only for a quick nod of my husband's approval...and that is exactly what he did.

Within 24 hours, we had our little, cheap (free!), and I might add, cute dog that I had been praying for. God is so good; He gives us exceedingly, abundantly more than we could think or ask for. When petitioning for a family pet, my prayers never included asking for a new collar or for our new dog to have all its current shots from the vet. However, the kind woman who brought us our new doggie provided both as a gift. Through the generosity of this woman, God added in all the bells and whistles for good measure.

God wants us to realize, comprehend, and appreciate the gifts of divine favor and blessing so freely and lavishly bestowed on us. More appropriately than naming her after a vacuum cleaner, we decided to name her Buttons because she truly was as cute as one. We had this precious dog for 17 years; she was such a sweet and dear companion to all of us.

Today, God is saying to each of us, "You've got mail," and we can be sure it's definitely not junk!

God can do anything, you know—far more than you could ever imagine or guess or request in your wildest dreams!
—Ephesians 3:20 MSG

"Dog is God spelled backward." —Duane Chapman

Prayer:

Lord, we marvel at Your delightful gifts You bestow on us. The blessings flow from Your hand in the most unexpected places. You never miss a beat when it comes to caring and providing for Your children. How we love You!

The Broken Buddha

My dad was famous for bringing things home when he was a traveling salesman. Sometimes this just meant he traveled back and forth to a local auto parts store where he worked. But no matter, he always seemed to find treasures to cart home. As I'm typing this, it dawned on me that I'm a lot like him. What an epiphany...it only took 61 years for this realization. Better late than never I always say.

When dad brought home fake decorative trees adorned with pink plastic flowers or burnt orange fall leaves, it was my mom's job to try to work his purchases into their home design while maintaining her own style. At times, this task proved to be a challenge.

However, hands down, the one item that was the most difficult and loathsome for my mother to incorporate (let alone bring into the house at all) was a gargantuan sized ceramic statue of Buddha—sporting both arms lifted high while His rotund belly protruded out unashamedly.

That newly acquired find not only didn't fit my mom's décor, it did not fit her Christian beliefs. So, with these two blaring conflicts, she quickly had Dad usher it downstairs to the farthest corner of the rec room...a time out of sorts for Mr. Buddha, perhaps chalking it up to his bad behavior. My mom was always good with a "work around" solution when it came to making a home for my dad's finds.

And while my dad's crazy Buddha statue had his perpetual time out in

134

the basement, there came a day when that find met his match with two young girls with too much energy and time on their hands. My dear childhood friend Janet and I were quite the pair. To be honest, I don't remember what our reasons were to go downstairs and engage with the statue on that fateful day, but I have no doubt we were caught up in the midst of some heightened wackiness for sure. It all our mayhem and merriment, all of the sudden, Mr. Buddha fell over and lost his arms! Those arms, once raised high, were now completely and cleanly sheared off from the impact, yet miraculously the arms remained totally intact. Unbelievable!

This smooth break from his tubby torso, was something no one could have replicated even if they tried. Believe you me, we did not try at all. Truth be told, I'm now 100 % convinced my mom's prayers for its demise were the culprit. That woman knew how to pray.

Janet and I were horrified at this mishap. I quickly sprang into action, darting upstairs for glue to apply a 911 emergency adhesive on the severed arms. Carefully gluing the ends, we attached his broken limbs to his body while propping them up with our hands. However, the moment we let go, gravity took over, causing them to slide down. We repeated this several times with the same end result. It was a dizzying and rather exhausting experience, as if the glue smell was not dizzying enough. In our desperate attempt to keep Buddha's arms on, the strong smell of glue wafted up the stairs, grabbing my mom's attention. Kicking into high gear, as any loving mother would do, she quickly walked down the stairs to investigate the cause of the intense fumes. Even though I was initially afraid of what her reaction would be, I was greatly relieved to see that for the very first time, my mom was actually happy that I had broken something.

This funny memory came to mind the other day and as I reminisced this event. I also pondered it.

I had just finished a story called Hidden Idols and how God brought about a Holy Spirit course correction into my life—a path of learning to trust Him more. And here I was again, pondering idols with a new revelation, and I felt the Lord say, "Lisa, what idols are you trying to prop up and save in your life?" I thought of one unhealthy relationship He had lovingly removed from my life or severed, but I was having a hard time letting go of it. For one, I thought I had broken it, so therefore I needed to fix it, wanting so badly to mend it when I was not called to do that anymore.

Truth is, it was just not meant to be. This happens sometimes in our lives, and no amount glue or human effort can prop it up. I'm reminded of Romans 12:18 NIV:

> *If it is possible, as far as it depends on you,*
> *live at peace with everyone.*

We need to do our best and leave the rest to God.

The other arm, if you will, was revealed days later when I thought how at times I can let my mind go idle. Though its spelled differently (idol/idle), it was still an effective way to get my attention.

The dictionary describes idle thoughts as *frivolous, trivial, minor, meaningless, and purposeless* to name a few.

I don't want to focus my energies on unnecessary or valueless thoughts that have no purpose. Instead, I choose to do what Philippians 4:8-9 MSG encourages us to do:

> *Summing it all up, friends, I'd say you'll do best by filling your*
> *minds and meditating on things true, noble, reputable, authentic,*
> *compelling, gracious—the best, not the worst; the beautiful, not the*
> *ugly; things to praise, not things to curse. Put into practice what*
> *you learned from me, what you heard and saw and realized. Do*
> *that, and God, who makes everything work together, will work you*
> *into his most excellent harmonies.*

As I looked at what could be another idol in my life, I repented of what I believed God was wanting to address and asked the Holy Spirit to keep me alert to any other idols in my life.

Because truthfully, there can be a lot of areas in our lives where idols can find their way into so many of our situations.

So, today I'm putting down the tube of glue; the glue of my own understanding and efforts that try to keep unhealthy or broken things together...when all along, these were actually God's "divine" and "clean" breaks.

A clean cut from an idol that's not supposed to be there in the first place is a good thing.

"I pray to know God and serve Him with a whole heart and with a willing mind, for You, LORD, search all hearts and understand every plan and thought" (1 Chronicles 28:9, my paraphrase).

Thank you, Lord Jesus, for breaking off any idols that have found a home in my heart.

"The Christian is an idol breaker." —Billy Graham

Getting Your Bearings

Ever have one of those terrible, horrible, no good, very bad days just like Alexander? Or at the very least, a day where you rolled out of bed, planting your feet firmly on the wrong side? Those are days when life seems off; your connection with God is lack luster, and the cares of the world are in an all-out brawl to swallow your joy. Even though I know God's Word tells us in Psalm 118:24 ESV, "This is the day that the Lord has made let us rejoice and be glad in it." Rejoicing in the midst of challenging circumstances takes work! Encountering days of all sunshine and roses presents easy-peasy rejoicing that effortlessly rolls off my tongue, opposed to rejoicing through hardship, setbacks, and disappointment. How I long to walk with more appreciation every single day, living in life's moments thanking God for what He offers me.

Allowing God's truths to create deep roots, it strengthens my trust in Him and chokes out the relentless worries that cloud His far grander purpose. Choosing to count it all joy, I calculate with heavenly mathematics rather than worldly equations. Bank on the truth that God is in the business of dividing our sorrows and multiplying our joys, turning our hardships into hallelujahs. God longs for us to possess these heartfelt desires in far greater dimensions than we could ever imagine.

God is ever so faithful to keep me on the right path. He reveals His deep and unfailing love even when I flounder in my faith, doubt Him, myself or a myriad of other things that can rob my joy and peace.

On one occasion, I felt that love in a tangible way—a hug to my heart from the throne room, delightfully bringing a touch of heaven on earth. On this particular stressful day, a series of circumstances led to an all-too-familiar and unwelcome companion: a burdensome yoke called "people pleasing," its pressure digging deep into my soul. Somehow this unwanted formidable foe snuck in the back door of my stressful day, hanging his hat on my weariness and his coat on my well-worn emotional peg, hoping to cozy up for a long stay.

A normally pleasant walk that day was suddenly turning unpleasant with my twirling mind of self-doubt! With each step, I wallowed in guilt and condemnation, forgoing even a glimmer of positive self-talk that could talk me off the ledge. At that point, positive self-talk seemed like too much extra work. Instead, I forged ahead and fell into a familiar, well-traveled rut that led me into a full-blown pity party! Heck, why not? I had already gotten the persuasive invitation.

Keeping my head down with no party hat in sight, I trudged up a hill while beads of perspiration collected on my furrowed brow. Just when my head felt like it could hang no lower without scraping on a tree root, all of the sudden I saw a glass marble nestled in the green grass. The beautiful, shiny, clear orb with a brilliant green swirl of color in the center absolutely stopped me in my tracks. I picked it up with delight. Giddy, I held it up with admiration; my heart flooded with childlike wonder as the weight of guilt and condemnation was exchanged for joy coming in the smallest form. After admiring this spherical wonder for several moments, I tucked it into my pocket while sensing the Lord lovingly saying to me, "Be childlike, Lisa, enjoy the moment, the beauty, and don't worry about pleasing people."

Like a tiny mustard seed telling a mountain to be cast into the sea, this tiny glass orb changed the atmosphere toward a richer love for God, myself, and others. It allowed me to refocus and enjoy the journey and its fresh, new perspective. All of that came in the tiniest of packages.

As glorious as this revelation was, I found myself in need of another teachable moment soon after. A few days later, I came home to see a fire truck and firemen hosing down a neighbor's house that evidently had been burning 15 mins prior. Though I was thankful to hear that everyone in their household was safe, including their pets, I was grieving for their loss. I also became sad and sentimental for our neighborhood of 24 yrs. For many years this particular house held fond memories of our boys' childhood friends who lived there. It held countless stories of five boys leaving their joyful mark on our little community with all their... ahem, "creativity." My heart was heavy as I walked to our son's house a block away, checking on it as a precautionary measure while he was on vacation.

Grappling with unsettled emotions, I tried to get my bearings in all this upheaval surrounding our neighborhood. Once again, I found myself gazing at the ground, head hung low, as I walked back home, when suddenly I saw a shiny ball bearing. I quickly picked it up only to walk a couple more steps and spotted another one, then another!

Ball bearings are known for allowing movement, while reducing friction and handling stress. This gentle reminder revealed that I had lost my "faith bearings." Stress, fear, and loss steered me off course from walking in His truth that God works out all things for good to those who love Him. God, in His patience and loving ways, lifted my spirits afresh in a tangible way to place in my pocket and nestle in my heart.

Are you tired? Worn out? Burned out on religion? Come to me. Get away with me and you'll recover your life. I'll show you how to take a real rest. Walk with me and work with me—watch how I do it. Learn the unforced rhythms of grace. I won't lay anything heavy or ill-fitting on you. Keep company with me and you'll learn to live freely and lightly. —Matthew 11:28–30 MSG

"Life is a journey to be experienced not a problem to be solved."
—Winnie the Pooh

"As the sailor locates his position on the sea by "shooting" the sun, so we may get our moral bearings by looking at God.
We must begin with God." —A.W. Tozer

Prayer:
Thank you, God, that You are the glory and the lifter of my head, and because of You, "...we walk with uplifted faces" Psalm 89:17 AMPC. May we find our bearings in You alone.

God's Grace for Every Season

 *Fall*

*So rejoice, O children of Zion, And delight in the LORD, your God;
For He has given you the early (autumn) rain in vindication And He
has poured down the rain for you, The early (autumn) rain and the
late (spring) rain, as before. And the threshing floors shall be full of
grain, and the vats shall overflow with new wine and oil.*
—Joel 2:23 AMP

"I loved autumn, the one season of the year that God seemed to have
put there just for the beauty of it." —Lee Maynard

Pocket Full of Promises

What has the Lord been showing you in this fall season?

_____

_____

_____

_____

_____

Write a one-word takeaway to describe this season.

_____

*Be patient, therefore, brothers, until the coming of the Lord. See how
the farmer waits for the precious fruit of the earth, being patient about
it, until it receives the early and the late rains.* —James 5:7 ESV

I'm single-minded in pursuit of you; don't let me miss the road signs you've posted. I've banked your promises in the vault of my heart so I won't sin myself bankrupt. Be blessed, GOD; train me in your ways of wise living... —Psalm 119:9-16 **MSG**

"The seasons change, and you change, but your Lord abides evermore the same, and the streams of His love are as deep, as broad, and as full as ever." —Charles Spurgeon

Connect with author Lisa Jennings at:

Lisa's blog: visit **LisaJenningsBooks.com**

Follow Lisa on Instagram: **@heartfulministries**

Connect with Lisa on Facebook: **Lisa Thompson Jennings**

Purchase Lisa's other books, including ***Reclaimed Joy, Reclaimed Joy Journal***, and the ***Clothed in Strength and Dignity: Cherishing and Coloring Through Proverbs*** on Amazon.

To contact Lisa with reader testimonials, interview requests or to book her for a speaking opportunity, contact her now at **lisathompsonjennings@gmail.com**

If you've enjoyed this book, please consider leaving *Grace-Filled Seasons* a positive review on Amazon and Goodreads!

Published with help from 100X Publishing: